# COPYRIGHT AND DISCLAIMER



Tim Wesley

I0503454

**Published by:**
Leader Publishing Worldwide
19 Axford Bay
Port Moody, BC V3H 3R4
Tel: 1 888 294 9151
Fax: 1 877 575 9151

DISCLAIMER AND/OR LEGAL NOTICES:
While every attempt has been made to verify information provided in this book, neither the author nor the publisher assumes any responsibility for any errors, omissions or inaccuracies.

Any slights of people or organizations are unintentional. If advice concerning legal or related matters is needed, the services of a qualified professional should be sought. This book is not intended as a source of legal or accounting advice. You should be aware of any laws which govern business transactions or other business practices in your state or province.

The income statements and examples are not intended to represent or guarantee that everyone will achieve the same results. Each individual's success will be determined by his or her desire, dedication, effort, and motivation. There are no guarantees you will duplicate the results stated here, you recognize that any business endeavor has inherent risk for loss of capital.

Any reference to any persons or business, whether living or deceased, existing or defunct, is purely coincidental.

PRINTED IN 2017

# Preface

Tim started his sales and marketing career in the Health, Wellness, and Fitness Industry. He has successfully transformed distressed fitness facilities and taken successful clubs to the next level of production. Tim has been able to create a proven process that has an established and tested track record for turning around suffering fitness businesses and taking successful companies to a level of profitability they never thought possible.

Tim's extensive experience in marketing, training and managing sales people and staff have been a key factor in the growth of fitness facilities nationwide.

Because of the success Tim has had with his proven marketing strategies and techniques, he has published his strategic marketing book, "S.H.O.C.K. Marketing," Strategies that Explode Fitness Business Revenue.

Tim's Consulting Company, TWfics Strategic Marketing, boasts a dynamic and proven Fitness Business Growth System that gives all fitness business owners and entrepreneurs the ability to cut through all the hype and B.S. and follow a proven step-by-step roadmap for turning your ideas into money... making your business' phone ring, herding prospects to your website, and successfully marketing your new or existing business.

Tim works directly with fitness business owners to implement his proven five-step formula:

**S.H.O.C.K.**

- Substantially increase lead generate
- Heighten Conversion of prospects to members
- Optimize and increase transactions per members
- Cost Reduction
- Keep Creating more profits

So, if you're struggling, or you're stuck and can't figure out how to grow past a certain point in your fitness business, it's not your fault. You were simply never taught the right way to separate yourself from your competition so you never have to compete on price or how to consistently bring in new members while getting your existing members to buy more and more often.

Tim shows fitness business owners and entrepreneurs how to out-think, out-market and out-sell their competition, and he has the unprecedented ability to find you a minimum of $10,000 hidden inside your business within 45 minutes... and without spending a cent on marketing or advertising.

When you're ready to take your fitness business to the next level and you'd like to know how to generate all the leads your business can handle without wasting money on advertising that doesn't work, then Tim Wesley's Strategic Marketing and Business Growth System is a MUST for you.

Email Tim at info@twfics.com or call 800-714-6067.

# Contents

# INTRODUCTION

When I put pen to paper or keyboard to word document, I found myself with an enormous amount of useful marketing material I've used since 1992. This experience is drawn from over 25 years working in the Fitness Industry years including Sales and Marketing Manager for numerous well known health clubs; ownership and management of my children's wellness center; and ownership of my fitness consulting company. Several of these companies I continue to own and consult to from afar. The strategies I talk about in this book are still in place at these companies.

Even though I truly believe we are all 1 or 2 great marketing ideas away from more sales opportunities than we can fully imagine, I believe the first two chapters are as important as the following eight. The strategies in this book - when implemented with strategy and care - are guaranteed to make you more money with less effort. These are strategies that have helped fitness centers just like yours make hundreds of thousands of dollars - including your competitors.

This is the reason I have dedicated my life to Business Consulting. Since starting my company to provide direction for fitness center operators, I have literally been overwhelmed with the demand for marketing campaigns, business structure, accountability programs, and the need for health club operators to surround themselves with someone that cares and provides a proper and profitable third party perspective.

As you follow this book and read the principles to follow, remember it does not matter type of fitness business you operate (I've been part of many). What matters is that you grasp the heart of the principles and the underlying lessons and strategies that can help grow any size and any type of fitness operation.

Yours in success,

-Tim Wesley

PS. If you would like to arrange a meeting to get a profitable third party perspective on your business, please send an email to info@twfics.com and we will gladly point you in the right direction.

For a Free Test Drive of all my best tips, tricks, and marketing resources visit www.shockexpert.com and www.ficonsult.net

# 1

# Define Your Target Market

## What is a Target Market?

Many fitness businesses can't answer the question: *Who is your target market?* They have often made the fatal assumption that *everyone* will want to purchase their product or service with the right marketing strategy.

A target market is simply the group of customers or clients who will purchase a specific product or service. This group of people all have something in common, often age, gender, hobbies, or location.

Your target market, then, are the people who will buy your offering. This includes both existing and potential customers, all of whom are motivated to do one of three things:

- Fulfill a need
- Solve a problem
- Satisfy a desire

To build, maintain, and grow your business, you need to know who your customers are, what they do, what they like, and why they would buy your product or service. Getting this wrong – or not taking the time to get it right – will cost you time, money, and potentially the success of your business.

## The Importance of Knowing Your Target Market

Knowledge and understanding of your target market is the keystone in the arch of your fitness business. Without it, your product or service positioning, pricing, marketing strategy, and eventually, your business could very quickly fall apart.

If you don't intimately know your target market, you run the risk of making mistakes when it comes to establishing pricing, product mix, or service packages. Your marketing strategy will lack direction, and produce mediocre results at best. Even if your marketing message and unique selling proposition (USP) are clear, and your brochure is perfectly designed, it means nothing unless it arrives in the hands (or ears) of the right people.

Determining your target market takes time and careful diligence. While it often starts with a best guess, assumptions cannot be relied on and research is required to confirm original ideas. Your target market is not always your ideal market.

Once you build an understanding of who your target market is, keep up with your market research. Having your finger on the pulse of their motivations and drivers – which naturally change – will help you to anticipate needs or wants and evolve your fitness business.

## Types of Markets

### Consumer

The Consumer Market includes those general consumers who buy products and services for personal use, or for use by family and friends. This is the market category you or I fall into when we're shopping for groceries or clothes, seeing a movie in the theatre, or going out for lunch. Retailers focus on this market category when marketing their goods or services.

### Institutional

The Institutional Market serves society and provides products or services for the benefit of society. This includes hospitals, non-profit organizations, government organizations, schools and universities. Members of the Institutional Market purchase products to use in the provision of services to people in their care.

### Business to Business (B2B)

The B2B Market is just what it seems to be: businesses that purchase the products and services of other business to run their operations. These purchases can include products that are used to manufacture other products (raw or technical), products that are needed for daily operations (such as office supplies), or services (such as accounting, shredding, and legal).

### Reseller

This market can also be called the "Intermediary Market" because it consists of businesses that act as channels for goods and services between other markets. Goods are purchased and sold for a profit – without any alterations. Members of this market include wholesalers, retailers, resellers, and distributors.

## Determining Your Target Market

### Product / Service Investigation

The process for determining your target market starts by examining exactly what your offering is, and what the average customer's motivation for purchasing it is.

Start by answering the following questions:

| | |
|---|---|
| **Does your offering meet a basic need?** | |
| **Does your offering serve a particular want?** | |
| **Does your offering fulfill a desire?** | |
| **What is the lifecycle of your product / service?** | |
| **What is the availability of your offering?** | |
| **What is the cost of the average customer's purchase?** | |
| **What is the lifecycle of your offering?** | |
| **How many times or how often will customers purchase your offering?** | |
| **Do you foresee any upcoming changes in your industry or region that may affect the sale of your offering (positive/negative)?** | |

**Market Investigation**

- **On the ground.** Spend some time on the ground researching who your target market might be. If you're thinking about opening a coffee shop, hang out in the neighborhood at different times of the day to get a sense of the people who live, work, and play in the neighborhood. Notice their age, gender, clothing, and any other indications of income and activities.
- **At the competition.** Who is your direct competitor targeting? Is there a small niche that is being missed? Observing the clientele of your competition can help to build understanding of your target market, regardless of whether it is the same or opposite. For example, if you own a children's clothing boutique and the majority of middle-class mothers shop at the local department store, you may wish to focus on higher-income families as your target market.
- **Online.** Many cities and towns – or at least regions – have demographic information available online. Research the ages, incomes, occupations, and other key pieces of information about the people who live in the area you operate your business. From this data, you will gain an understanding of the size of your total potential market.
- **With existing members.** Talk to your existing members through focus groups or surveys. This is a great way to gather demographic and behavioral information, as well as genuine feedback about product or service quality and other information that will be useful in a business or marketing strategy.

**Who is Your Market?**

Based on your product / service and market investigations, you will be able to piece together a basic picture of your target market, and some of their general characteristics. Record some notes here. At this point, you may wish to be as specific as possible, or maintain some generalities. You can further segment your market in the next section.

## Consumer Target Market Framework

| | |
|---|---|
| **Market Type:** | **Consumer** |
| **Gender:** | ☐ Male ☐ Female |
| **Age Range:** | |
| **Purchase Motivation:** | ☐ Meet a Need<br>☐ Serve a Want<br>☐ Fulfill a Desire |
| **Activities:** | |
| **Income Range:** | |
| **Marital Status:** | |
| **Location:** | ☐ Neighborhood ☐ Region<br>☐ City ☐ Country |
| **Other Notes:** | |

## Institutional Target Market Framework

| **Market Type:** | **Institutional** |
| --- | --- |
| **Institution Type:** | ☐ Hospital<br>☐ School<br>☐ Charity<br>☐ Church<br>☐ Non-profit<br>☐ University<br>☐ Government |
| **Purchase Motivation:** | ☐ Operational Need<br>☐ Client Want<br>☐ Client Desire |
| **Purpose of Institution:** | |
| **Institution's Client Base:** | |
| **Size:** | |
| **Location:** | ☐ Neighborhood<br>☐ City<br>☐ Region<br>☐ County |
| **Other Notes:** | |

## B2B Target Market Framework

| | |
|---|---|
| **Market Type:** | Business to Business (B2B) |
| **Company Size:** | |
| **Number of Employees:** | |
| **Purchase Motivation:** | ☐ Operations Need<br>☐ Strategy<br>☐ Functionality |
| **Annual Revenue:** | |
| **Industry:** | |
| **Location(s):** | |
| **Purpose of Business:** | |
| **People, Culture & Values:** | |
| **Other Notes:** | |

## Reseller Target Market Framework

| **Market Type:** | **Reseller** |
|---|---|
| **Industry:** | |
| **Client Base:** | |
| **Purchase Motivation:** | ☐ Operations Need<br>☐ Client Wants<br>☐ Functionality |
| **Annual Revenue:** | |
| **Age:** | |
| **Location:** | ☐ Neighborhood<br>☐ Region<br>☐ City<br>☐ Country |
| **Other Notes:** | |

## Your Target Market: Putting It Together

Based on the information you gather from your product / service and market investigations, you should have a clear vision of your realistic target market. Here are a few examples of how this information is put together and conclusions are drawn:

## Target Market Sample 1: Consumer Market

<table>
<tr><td>Business: Baby Clothing Boutique</td><td rowspan="4">Business Purpose:<br>Meet a need (provide clothing for infants and children aged 0 to 5 years). Serve a want (clothing is brand name only, and has a higher price point than the competition).</td></tr>
<tr><td>Market Type: Consumer</td></tr>
<tr><td>Gender: Women</td></tr>
<tr><td>Marital Status: Married</td></tr>
<tr><td>Market Observations:<br>located on Main Street of Anytown, a street that is seeing many new boutiques open up, proximate to the main shopping mall two blocks from popular mid-range restaurant that is busy at lunch</td><td>Industry Predictions:<br>large number of new housing developments in the city and surrounding areas two new schools in construction expect to see an influx of new families move to town from Anycity</td></tr>
<tr><td>Competition Observations:<br>baby clothing also available at two local department stores, and one second-hand shop on opposite side of town</td><td>Online Research:<br>half of Anytown's population is female, and 25% have children under the age of 15 years Anytown's population is expected to increase by 32% within three years. The average household income for Anytown is $75,000 annually</td></tr>
<tr><td colspan="2">TARGET MARKET: The target market can then be described as married mothers with children under five years old, between the ages of 25 and 45, who have recently moved to Anytown from Anycity, and have a household income of at least $100K annually.</td></tr>
</table>

## Target Market Sample 2: B2B Market

| | |
|---|---|
| **Business:** Confidential Paper Shredding | **Target Business Size:** Small to medium |
| **Market Type:** B2B (Business to Business) | **Target Business Revenue:** $500K to $1M |
| **Business Purpose:**<br>*Meet an operations need* (provide confidential on-site shredding services for business documents) | **Target Business Type:**<br>produce or handle a variety of sensitive paper documentation accountants, lawyers, real estate agents, etc. |
| **Market Observations:**<br>there are two main areas of office buildings and industrial warehouses in Anycity three more office towers are being constructed, and will be completed this year | **Industry Predictions:**<br>the professional sector is seeing revenue growth of 24% over last year, which indicates increased client billing and staff recruitment |
| **Competition Observations:**<br>one confidential shredding company serves the region, covering Anycity and the surrounding towns provide regular (weekly or biweekly) service, but does not have the capacity to handle large volumes at one time | **Online Research:**<br>Anycity's biggest employment sectors are: manufacturing, tourism, food services, and professional services |
| **TARGET MARKET:**<br>The target market can then be described as small to medium sized businesses in the professional sector with an annual revenue of $500K to $1M who require both regular and infrequent large volume paper shredding services. | |

## Segmenting Your Market

Your market segments are the groups within your target market – broken down by a determinant in one of the following four categories:

- Demographics
- Psychographics
- Geographics
- Behaviors

Segmenting your target market into several more specific groups allows you to further tailor your marketing campaign and more specifically position your product or service. You may wish to divide your ad campaign into four sections, and target four specific markets with messages that will most resonate with the audience.

For example, the baby clothing store may choose to segment its target market by psychographics, or lifestyle. If the larger target market is *married females with children under five, between the ages of 25 and 45, who have a household income of at least $100K annually*, it can be broken down into the following lifestyle segments:

- Fitness-oriented mothers
- Career-oriented mothers
- New mothers

With these three categories, unique marketing messages can be created that speak to the hot-buttons of each segment. The more accurate and specific you can make communications with your target market, the greater impact you will have on your revenues.

## Market Segmentation Variables

| Demographic | Psychographic | Geographic | Behavioristic |
|---|---|---|---|
| Age Income<br>Gender<br>Generation<br>Nationality<br>Ethnicity<br>Marital Status<br>Family Size<br>Occupation<br>Religion<br>Language<br>Education<br>Employment Type<br>Housing Type<br>Housing<br>Ownership<br>Political<br>Affiliation | Personality<br>Lifestyle<br>Values<br>Attitude<br>Motivation<br>Activities<br>Interests | Region<br>Country<br>City<br>Area<br>Neighborhood<br>Density<br>Climate | Brand Loyalty<br>Product Usage<br>Purchase<br>Frequency<br>Profitability<br>Readiness to Buy<br>User Status |

## Understanding Your Target Market

Once you have determined who your market is, make a point of learning everything you can about them. You need to have a strong understanding of who they are, what they like, where they shop, why they buy, and how they spend their time. Remind yourself that you may *think* you know your market, but until you have verified the information, you'll be driving your marketing strategy blind.

Also be aware that markets change, just like people. Just because you knew your market when you started your business 10 years ago, doesn't mean you know it now. Regular market research is part of any successful business plan, and a great habit to start.

## Types of Market Research

### Surveys

The simplest way to gather information from your clients or target market is through a survey. You can craft a questionnaire full of questions about your product, service, market demographics, buyer motivations, and so on. Plus, anonymous surveys will produce the most accurate information since names are not attached to the results or specific comments.

Depending on the purpose—whether it is to gather demographic information, product or service feedback, or other data—there are a number of ways to administer a survey.

1. *Telephone*

Telephone surveys are a more time-consuming option, but have the benefit of live communication with your target market. Generally, it is best to have a third party conduct this type of survey to gather the most honest feedback. This is the method that market researchers use for polling, which is highly reliable.

2. *Online*

Online surveys are the easiest to administer yourself. There a many web-based services that quickly and easily allow you to custom create your survey, and send it to your email marketing list. These services can also analyze, summarize and interpret the results on your behalf. Keep in mind that the results include only those who are motivated to respond, which may slant your results.

3. *Paper*

Paper surveys are seldom used, and can prove to be an inefficient method. Like online surveys, your results are based on the feedback of those who were motivated for one reason or another to respond. However, the time and effort involved in taking the survey, filing it out, and returning it to your place of business may deter people from participating.

Keep in mind that surveys can be complex to administer, and consume more time and resources than you have planned. If you have the budget, consider hiring a professional market research firm to lead or assist with the process. This will also ensure that the methodology is standard practice, and will garner the most accurate results.

**Website Analysis**

Tracking your website traffic is an excellent way to research your existing and potential customer's interests and behavior. From this information, you can ensure the design, structure and content of your website is catering to the people who use it – and the people you want to use it.

User-friendly website traffic analytics programs can easily show you who is visiting your site, where they are from, and what pages of your site they are viewing. Services like Google Analytics can tell you what page they arrive at, where they click to, how much time they spend on each page, and on which page they leave the site.

This is powerful (and free!) information to have in your market research, and easy to monitor monthly or weekly, depending on the needs of your business.

**Customer Purchase Data (Consumer Behavior)**

If you do not have the budget to conduct your own professional market research, you can use existing resources on consumer behavior. While this data may not be specific to your region or city, general consumer research is actual data that can be helpful in confirming assumptions you may have made about your target market.

Your customer loyalty program or Point of Sale system may also be of help in tracking customer purchases and identifying trends in purchase behavior. If you can track who is buying, what they're buying and how often they're buying, you'll have an arsenal of powerful insight into your existing client base.

**Focus Groups**

Focus groups look at the psychographic and behavioristic aspects of your target market. Groups of six to 12 people are gathered and asked general and specific questions about their purchase motivations and behaviors. These questions could relate to your business in particular, or to the general industry.

Focus group sessions can also be time consuming to organize and facilitate, so consider hiring the services of a professional market research firm. You may also receive more honest information if a third party is asking the questions, and receiving the responses from focus group participants.

For cost savings, consider partnering with an associate in the same industry who is not a direct competitor, and who would benefit from the same market data.

# 2

# Creating a Powerful Offer

I'm not going to beat around the bush on this one:

*Your offer is the granite foundation of your marketing campaign.*

Get it right, and everything else will fall into place. our headline will grab readers, your copy will sing, your ad layout will hardly matter, and you will have customers running to your door.

Get it wrong, and even the best looking, best-written campaign will sink like the Titanic.

A powerful offer is an irresistible offer. It's an offer that gets your audience frothing at the mouth and clamoring over each other all the way to your door. n offer that makes your readers pick up the phone and open their wallets.

Irresistible offers make your potential customers think, "I'd be crazy not to take him up on that," or "An offer like this doesn't come around very

often." They instill a sense of emotion, of desire, and ultimately, urgency.

Make it easy for customers to purchase from you the first time, and spend your time keeping them coming back.

I'll say it again: **get it right, and everything else will fall into place.**

## The Crux of Your Marketing Campaign

As you work your way through this program, you will find that nearly every chapter discusses the importance of a powerful offer as related to your marketing strategy or promotional campaign.

There's a reason for this. The powerful offer is more often than not the reason a customer will open their wallets. It is how you generate leads, and then convert them into loyal customers. The more dramatic, unbelievable, and valuable the offer is the more dramatic and unbelievable the response will be.

Many companies spend thousands of dollars on impressive marketing campaigns in glossy magazines and big city newspapers. They send massive direct mail campaigns on a regular basis; yet don't receive an impressive or massive response rate.

These companies do not yet understand that simply providing information on their company and the benefits of their product is not enough to get customers to act. There is no reason to pick up the phone or visit the store, *right now*.

Your powerful, irresistible offer can:

- Increase leads
- Drive traffic to your website or business
- Move old product
- Convert leads into customers
- Build your customer database

## What Makes a Powerful Offer?

A powerful offer is one that makes the most people respond, and take action. It gets people running to spend money on your product or service.

Powerful offers nearly always have an element of *urgency* and of *scarcity*. They give your audience a reason to act immediately, instead of put it off until a later date.

Urgency relates to time. The offer is only available until a certain date, during a certain period of the day, or if you act within a few hours of seeing the ad. The customer needs to act now to take advantage of the offer.

Scarcity related to quantity. There are only a certain number of customers who will be able to take advantage of the offer. There may be a limited number of spaces, a limited number of products, or simply a limited number of people the business will provide the offer to. Again, this requires that customer acts immediately to reap the high value for low cost.

Powerful offers also:

**Offer great value.** Customers perceive the offer as having great value – more than a single product on its own, or the product at its regular price. It is clear that the offer takes the reader's needs and wants into consideration.

**Make sense to the reader.** They are simple and easy to understand if read quickly. Avoid percentages – use half off or 2 for 1 instead of 50% off. There are no "catches" or requirements; no fine print.

**Seem logical.** The offer doesn't come out of thin air. There is a logical reason behind it – a holiday, end of season, anniversary celebration, or new product. People can get suspicious of offers that seem "too good to be true" and have no apparent purpose.

**Provide a premium.** The offer provides something extra to the customer, like a free gift, or free product or service. They feel they are getting something extra for no extra cost. Premiums are perceived to have more value than discounts.

**Remember that when your target market reads your offer, they will be asking the following questions:**

1. What are you offering me?
2. What's in it for me?
3. What makes me sure I can believe you?
4. How much do I have to pay for it?

## The Most Powerful Types of Offers

Decide what kind of offer will most effectively achieve your objectives. Are you trying to generate leads, convert customers, build a database, move old product off the shelves, or increase sales?

Consider what type of offer will be of most value to your ideal customers – what offer will make them act quickly.

### Free Offer

This type of offer asks customers to act immediately in exchange for something free. This is a good strategy to use to build a customer database or mailing list. Offer a free consultation, free consumer report, or other item of low cost to you but of high perceived value.

You can also advertise the value of the item you are offering for free. For example, act now and you'll receive a free consultation, worth $75 dollars. This will dramatically increase your lead generation, and allow you to focus on conversion when the customer comes through the door or picks up the phone.

### The Value Added Offer

Add additional services or products that cost you very little, and combine them with other items to increase their attractiveness. This increases the perception of value in the customer's mind, which will justify increasing the price of a product or service without incurring extra hard costs to your business.

**Package Offer**

Package your products or services together in a logical way to increase the perceived value as a whole. Discount the value of the package by a small margin, and position it as a "start-up kit" or "special package." By packaging goods of mixed values, you will be able to close more high- value sales. For example: including a free desk-jet printer with every computer purchase.

**Premium Offer**

Offer a bonus product or service with the purchase of another. This strategy will serve your bottom line much better than discounting. This includes 2 for 1 offers, offers that include free gifts, and in-store credit with purchases over a specific dollar amount.

**Urgency Offer**

As I mentioned above, offers that include an element of urgency enjoy a better response rate, as there is a reason for your customers to act immediately. Give the offer a deadline or limit the number of spots available.

**Guarantee Offer**

Offer to take the risk of making a purchase away from your customers. Guarantee the performance or results of your product or service, and offer to compensate the customer with their money back if they are not satisfied. This will help overcome any fear or reservations about your product, and make it more likely for your leads to become customers.

## Create Your Powerful Offer

**1. Pick a single product or service.**

Focus on only one product or service – or one product or service type – at a time. This will keep your offer clear, simple, and easy to understand. This can be an area of your business you wish to grow, or old product that you need to move off the shelves.

**2. Decide what you want your prospects to do.**

What are you looking to achieve from your offer? If it is to generate more leads, then you'll need your customer to contact you. If it is to quickly sell old product, you'll need your customer to come into the store and buy it. Do you want them to visit your website? Sign up for your newsletter? How long do they have to act? Be clear about your call to action, and state it clearly in your offer.

**3. Dream up the biggest, best offer.**

First, think of the biggest, best things you could offer your customers – regardless of cost and ability. Don't limit yourself to a single type of offer, combine several types of offers to increase value. Offer a premium, plus a guarantee, with a package offer. Then take a look at what you've created, and make the necessary changes so it is realistic.

**4. Run the numbers.**

Finally, make sure the offer will leave you with some profit – or at least allow you to break even. You don't want to publish an outrageous offer that will generate a tremendous number of leads, but leave you broke. Remember that each customer has an acquisition cost, as well as a lifetime value. The amount of their first purchase may allow you to break even, but the amount of their subsequent purchases may make you a lovely profit.

# 3

# Generating an Unlimited Amount of Leads for Your Fitness Business

Where do your fitness customers come from?

Most people would probably choose advertising as an answer. Or referrals. Or direct mail campaigns. This may seem true, but it's not really accurate.

Your customers come from leads that have been turned into sales. Each customer goes through a two-step process before they arrive with their wallets open. They have been converted from a member of a target market, to a lead, then to a customer.

So, would it not stand to reason then, that when you advertise or send any marketing material out to your target market, that you're not really trying to generate customers? That instead, you're trying to generate leads.

When you look at your marketing campaign from this perspective, the idea of generating leads as compared to customers seems a lot less daunting. The pressure of closing sales is no longer placed on advertisements or brochures.

From this perspective, the **general purpose of your advertising and marketing efforts is then to generate leads from qualified prospects.** Seems easy enough, doesn't it?

## Where Are Your Leads Coming From?

If I asked you to tell me the top three ways you generate new sales leads, what would you say?

- Advertising?
- Word of mouth?
- Networking?
- ...don't know?

The first step toward increasing your leads is in understanding how many leads you currently get on a regular basis, as well as where they come from. Otherwise, how will you know when you're getting more phone calls or walk-in customers?

If you don't know where your leads come from, start *today.* Start asking every customer that comes through your door, "how did you hear about us?" or "what brought you in today?" Ask every prospect that calls where they found your telephone number, or email address. Then, *record the information for at least an entire week.*

When you're finished, take a look at your spreadsheet and write your top three lead generators here:

1. ______________________________________________

2. ______________________________________________

3. ______________________________________________

## From Lead to Member: Conversion Rates

Leads mean nothing to your business unless you convert them into clients. You could get hundreds of leads from a single advertisement, but unless those leads result in purchases, it's been a largely unsuccessful (and costly) campaign.

The ratio of leads (potential customers) to transactions (actual customers) is called your conversion rate. Simply divide the number of customers who actually purchased something by the number of customers who inquired about your product or service, and multiply by 100.

**# transactions / # leads x 100 = % conversion rate**

If, in a given week, I have 879 customers come into my store, and 143 of them purchase something, the formula would look like this:

**[143 (customers) / 879 (leads)] x 100 = 16.25% conversion rate**

### What's Your Conversion Rate?

Based on the formula above, you can see that the higher your conversion rate, the more profitable the business.

Your next step is to determine you own current conversion rate. Add up the number of leads you sourced in the last section, and divide that number into the total transactions that took place in the same week.

Write your conversion rate here:

______________________________.

## Quality (or Qualified) Leads

Based on our review of conversion rates, we can see that the number of leads you generate means nothing unless those leads are being converted into customers.

So what affects your ability (and the ability of your team) to turn leads into customers? Do you need to improve your scripts? Your product or service? Find a more competitive edge in the marketplace?

Maybe. But the first step toward increasing conversion rates is to evaluate the leads you are currently generating, and make sure those leads are the right ones.

## What are Quality Leads?

Potential customers are potential customers, right? Anyone who walks into your store or picks up the phone to call your business could be convinced to purchase from you, right? Not necessarily, but this is a common assumption most business owners make.

Quality leads are the people who are the most likely to buy your product or service. They are the qualified buyers who comprise your target market. Anyone might walk in off the street to browse a furniture store – regardless of whether or not they are in the market for a new couch or bed frame. This lead is solely interested in browsing, and is not likely to be converted to customer.

A quality lead would be someone looking for a new kitchen table, and who specifically drove to that same furniture because a friend had raved about the service they received that month. **These are the kinds of leads you need to focus on generating.**

### How Do You Get Quality Leads?

- **Know your target market**. Get a handle on who your customers are – the people who are most likely to buy your product or service. Know their age, sex, income, and purchase motivations. With this information you can determine how best to reach your specific audience.

- **Focus on the 80/20 rule.** A common statistic in business is that 80% of your revenue comes from 20% of your customers. These are your star clients, or your ideal clients. These are the clients you should focus your efforts on recruiting. This is the easiest way to grow your business and your income.
- **Get specific.** Focus not only on who you want to attract, but how you're going to attract them. If you're trying to generate leads from a specific market segment, craft a unique offer to get their attention.
- **Be proactive**. Once you've generated a slew of leads, make sure you have the resources to follow up on them. Be diligent and aggressive, and follow up in a timely manner. You've done to work to get them, now reel them in.

## Get More Leads from Your Existing Strategies

Increasing your lead generation doesn't necessarily mean diving in and implementing an expensive array of new marketing strategies. Marketing and customer outreach for the purpose of lead generation can be inexpensive, and bring a high return on investment.

You are likely already implementing many of these strategies. With a little tweaking or refinement, you can easily double your leads, and ensure they are more qualified.

Here are some popular ways to generate quality leads:

### Direct Mail to Your Ideal Members

Direct mail is one of the fastest and most effective ways to generate leads that will build your business. It's a simple strategy – in fact, you're probably already reaching out to potential clients through direct mail letters with enticing offers.

The secret to doubling your results is to craft your direct mail campaigns specifically for a highly targeted audience of your *ideal* customers.

Your ideal customers are the people who will buy the most of your products or services. They are the customers who will buy from you over and over again, and refer your business to their friends. They are the group of 20% of your clients who make up 80% of your revenue.

**Identify your ideal members**

Who are your ideal members? What is their age, sex, income, location and purchase motivation? Where do they live? How do they spend their money? Be as specific as possible.

Once you have identified who your ideal members are, you can begin to determine how you can go about reaching them. Will you mail to households or apartment buildings? Families or retirees? Direct mail lists are available for purchase from a wide range of companies, and can be segregated into a variety of demographic and sociographic categories.

**Craft a special offer**

Create an offer that's too good to refuse – not for your entire target market, but for your ideal customer. How can you cater to their unique needs and wants? What will be irresistible for them?

For example, if you operate a furniture store, your target market is a broad range of people. However, if you are targeting young families, your offer will be much different than one you may craft for empty-nesters.

**Court them for their business**

Don't stop at a single mail-out. Sometimes people will throw your letter away two or three times before they are motivated to act. Treat your direct mail campaign like a courtship, and understand that it will happen over time.

First send a letter introducing yourself, and your irresistible offer. Then follow up on a monthly basis with additional letters, newsletters, offers, or flyers. Repetition and reinforcement of your presence is how your customer will go from saying, "who is this company" to "I buy from this company."

**Advertise for lead generation**

Statistics show that nearly 50% of all purchase decisions are motivated by advertising. It can also be a relatively cost effective way of generating leads.

We've already discussed the importance of ensuring your advertisements are purpose-focused. The general purpose of most advertisements is to increase sales – which starts with leads. However, ads that are created solely for lead generation – that is, to get the customers to pick up the phone or walk into the club – are a category of their own.

Lead generation ads are simply designed and create a sense of curiosity or mystery. Often, they feature an almost unbelievable offer. Their purpose is not to convince the customer to buy, but to contact the business for more information.

As always, when you are targeting your ideal audience, you'll need to ensure that your ads are placed prominently in publications that audience reads. This doesn't mean you have to fork over the cash for expensive display ads. Inexpensive advertising in e-mail newsletters, classifieds, and the yellow pages are very effective for lead generation.

Here are some tips for lead generation advertising:

**Leverage low-cost advertising**

Place ads in the yellow pages, classifieds section, e-mail newsletters, and online. If your target audience is technology savvy, consider new forms of advertising like Facebook and Google AdWords.

**Spark curiosity**

Don't give them all the information they need to make a decision. Ask them to contact you for the full story, or the complete details of the seemingly outrageous offer.

**Grab them with a killer headline**

Like all advertising, a compelling headline is essential. Focus on the greatest benefits to the customer, or feature an unbelievable offer.

**Referrals and host beneficiary relationships**

A referral system is one of the most profitable systems you can create in your fitness business. The beauty is once it's set up, it often runs itself.

Customers that come to you through referrals are often your "ideal customers." They are already trusting and willing to buy. This is one of the most cost-effective methods of generating new business, and is often the most profitable. These referral clients will buy more, faster, and refer further business to your fitness center.

Referrals naturally happen without much effort for reputable businesses, but with a proactive referral strategy you'll certainly double or triple your referrals. Sometimes, you just need to ask!

Here are some easy strategies you can begin to implement today:

**Referral incentives**

Give your members a reason to refer business to you. Reward them with discounts, gifts, or free service in exchange for a successful referral.

**Referral program**

Offer new members a free product or service to get them in the door. Then, at the end of the transaction, give them three more 'coupons' for the same free product or service that they can give to their friends. Do the same with their friends. This ongoing program will bring you more business than you can imagine.

### Host-beneficiary relationships

Forge alliances with non-competitive companies who target your ideal customers. Create cross-promotion and cross-referral direct mail campaigns that benefit both businesses.

## Lead Management Systems

Once your lead generation strategies are in place, you'll also need a system to manage incoming inquiries. You'll need to ensure you receive enough information from each lead to follow up on at a later date. You'll also need to create a system to organize that information, and track the lead as it is converted into a sale.

### Gathering Information from Your Leads

Here is a list of information you should gather from your leads. This list can be customized to the needs of your fitness business, and the type of information you can realistically ask for from your potential customers.

- Company Name
- Name of Contact
- Alternate Contact Person
- Mailing Address
- Phone Number
- Fax Number
- Cell Phone
- Email Address
- Website Address

- Product of Interest
- Other Competitors Engage

**Lead List Management Methods:**

Once you have gathered information from your lead, you'll need a system to organize their information and keep a detailed contact history.

The simplest way to do this is with a database program, but you can also use a variety of hard copy methods.

**Electronic Database Programs**

- High level of organization available
- Unlimited space for notes and record-keeping
- Data-entry required
- Examples include: MS Outlook, MS Excel, Maximizer
- Customer Relationship Management Software

**Index Cards**

- Variety of sizes: 3x5, 4X6 or 5X8
- Basic contact information on one side
- Notes on the other side
- Easy to organize and sort

**Rolodex System**

- Maintain more contacts than index card system
- Easily organized and compact
- Basic contact information on one side
- Notes on the other side
- Can keep phone conversation and purchase details

**Notebook**

- Best if leads are managed by a single person
- Lots of room for notes

- Inexpensive
- Difficult to re-organize
- Best for smaller lists

**Business Card Organizer**

- Best for small lists – under 100
- Limited space for notes
- No data entry required
- Rolodex-style, or clear binder pages

# 4

# Immediate Sales

If you own a fitness business, you're also a salesperson.

You've had to sell the bank to get them to loan you your start-up capital. You've had to sell the best employees on why they should work for your business. You've had to convince your business partner, spouse, and friends why your fitness business idea is a good one.

Now you have to repeatedly sell your product or service to your members.

The ability to sell effectively and efficiently is one every successful business owner has cultivated, and continues to develop. It can be a complicated and time consuming task; one that you will have to continually work on throughout your career in order to be – and stay – successful.

Fortunately, making sales is a step-by-step process that can be learned, customized, and continuously improved. There are a wide range of tools available to help and support your sales efforts.

You don't have to be the most outgoing, enthusiastic person to be successful at sales. You don't even have to be a good public speaker. All you need is an understanding of the basic sales process, and a genuine passion for what you are selling.

## Sales 101

As I said before, making sales is a process. There are clear, step-by- step actions that can be taken and result in a sale.

The sales process varies according to the type of business, type of customers and type of product or service that is offered; however, the core steps are the same. Similarly, sales training varies from individual to individual, but the core skills and abilities remain the same.

Here is a basic seven-step process that you can follow, or fine tune to suit your unique products and services. Remember that each step is important, and builds on the step previous. It is essential to become adept at each step, instead of solely focusing on closing the sale.

### 1. Preparation

Make sure you have prepared for your meeting, presentation, or day on the sales floor. You have complete control of this part of the sales process, so it is important to do everything you can to set the stage for your success.

- Understand your product or service inside and out.
- Prepare all the necessary materials, and organize them neatly.
- Keep your place of business tidy and organized. Reface product on shelves.
- Ensure you appear professional and well groomed.
- Do some research on your potential client and brainstorm to find common ground.

### 2. Build a Relationship

The first few minutes you spend with a potential customer set the stage for the rest of your interaction. First impressions are everything. Your goal in the second step is to relax the customer and begin to develop a relationship with them. Establishing a real relationship with your customer will create trust.

- Make a great first impression: shake hands, make eye contact, and introduce yourself.
- Remain confident and professional, but also personable.
- Mirror their speech and behavior.
- Begin with general questions and small talk.
- Show interest in them and their place of business.
- Notice and comment on positives.
- Find some common ground on which to relate.

**3. Discuss Needs + Wants**

Once you have spent a few moments getting to know your prospect, start asking open-ended questions to discover some of their needs and wants. If they have come to you on the sales floor, ask what brought them in the store. If you are meeting them to present your product or service, ask why they are interested in, or what criteria they have in mind for that product or service.

- If you are making a sales presentation, ask for a few moments at the outset to outline the purpose of your visit, as well as how you have structured the presentation.
- Listen intently, and repeat back information you are not sure you understand.
- Ask open-ended questions to get them talking. The longer they talk, the more insight they are providing you into their needs and purchase motivations.
- Ask clarifying questions about their responses.

- If you become sure the customer is going to buy your product or service, begin to ask questions specific to the offering. i.e., what size/color do you prefer?

**4. Present the Solution**

Once you have a solid understanding of what they are looking for, or what issue they are looking to resolve, you can begin to present the solution: your product or service.

- Explain how your product or service will solve their problem or meeting their needs. If several products apply, begin by presenting the mid-level product.
- Illustrate your points with anecdotes about other happy customers, or awards the product or service has earned.
- Use hypothetical examples featuring your customer. Encourage them to picture a scenario after their purchase.
- Begin by describing the benefits of the product, then follow up with features and advantages.
- Watch your customer's behavior as you speak, and ask further qualifying questions in response to body language and verbal comments.
- Give the customer an opportunity to ask you questions or provide feedback about each product or service after you have described or explained it.
- Ask closed-ended questions to gain agreement.

**5. Overcome Objections**

As you present the product or service, take note of potential objections by asking open-ended questions and monitoring body language. Expect that objections will arise and prepare for it. Consider brainstorming a list of all potential objections, and writing down your responses.

- Repeat the objection back to the customer to ensure you understand them correctly.
- Empathize with what they have said, and then provide a response that overcomes the objection.
- Confirm that the answer you have provided has overcome their objection by repeating yourself.

| **The Eight Most Common Objections** |
| --- |
| The product or service does not seem valuable to me. |
| There is no reason for me to act know. I will wait. |
| It's safest not to make a decision right away. |
| There is not enough money for the purchase. |
| The competitor or another department offers a better product. |
| There are internal issues between people or departments. |
| The relationship with the decision maker is strained. |
| There is an existing contract in place with another fitness business. |

**6. Close**

This is an important part of the sales process that should be handled delicately. Deciding when to close is a judgment call that must be made in the moment during the sale. Ideally, you have presented a solution to their problem, overcome objections, and have the customer in a place where they are ready to buy.

Here are some questions to ask before you close the sale:

- Does my prospect agree that there is value in my product or service?

- Does my prospect understand the features and benefits of the product or service?
- Are there any remaining objections that must be handled?
- What other factors could influence my prospect's decision to buy?
- Have I minimized the risk involved in the purchase, and provided some level of urgency?

Once you have determined it is time to make the sale, here are some sample statements you can use to get the process rolling:

- So, should we get started?
- Shall I grab a new one from the back?
- If you just give me your credit card, I can take care of the transaction while you meet our Fitness Director to set up your first appointment.
- We can begin next month if we receive payment by the end of the week.
- Can I email you a draft contract tomorrow?

**7. Service + Follow-up**

Once you have made the sale, your work is not over. You want to ensure that that customer will become a loyal, repeat customer, and that they will refer their friends to your fitness business.

Ask them to be in your customer database, and keep in touch with regular newsletters. Follow up with a phone call or drop by to ask how they are enjoying the product or service, and if they have any further questions or needs you can assist them with.

This contact opportunity will also allow you ask for a referral, or an up sell. At the very least, it will ensure you are continuing to foster and build a relationship with the member.

## Up selling

Up selling is simply inviting your members to spend more money in your fitness business by purchasing additional products or services. This could include more of the same product, complementary products, or impulse items.

Regardless, up selling is an effective way to increase profits and create loyal members – without spending any money to acquire the business. These members are already purchasing from you – which means they perceive value in what you have to offer – so take the information you have gained in the sales process and offer them a little bit more.

You experience up selling on a daily basis. From "do you want fries with that?" to "have you heard about our product protect program?" companies across the globe have tapped into and trained their staff on the value of the up sell.

Up selling is truly rooted in good customer service. If your client purchases a new computer printer, you'll need to make sure they have the cords required to connect it to the computer, regular and photo paper, and color and black and white ink.

If you don't suggest these items, they may arrive home and realize they do not have all the materials needed to use the product. They may choose to purchase those materials somewhere closer, cheaper, or more helpful.

Member education is another form of up selling. What if your member doesn't realize that you offer a variety of small group training programs as well as one-on-one personal training? Take every opportunity to educate your customer on the products and services you offer that may be of interest to them.

An effective way of implementing an up sell system into your fitness business is simply by creating add-on checklists for the products or services you offer. Each item has a list of related items that your customer may need. This will encourage your staff to develop the habit of asking for the up sell.

Other up sell strategies can be implemented:

- **At the point of sale**. This is a great place for impulse items like candy, flashlights, nail scissors, etc.
- **In a newsletter**. This is an effective strategy for member education.
- **In your merchandising**. Place strips of impulse items near related items.
- **Over the phone**. If someone is considering coming into your fitness center, ask them to bring a friend or family member.
- **With new products**. Feature each new product or service that you offer prominently in your fitness business, and ask your staff to mention it to every customer.

## Sales Team

Employing a team of strong salespeople

### What Makes a Good Salesperson?

There are a lot of salespeople out there – but what qualities and skills make a great salesperson? These are the attributes you will want to find or develop in your team:

- Willingness to continuously learn and improve sales skills

- Sincerity in relating to members and prospects and providing solutions to their objectives
- An understanding of the company's big picture
- A communication style that is direct, polite, and professional
- Honesty and respect for other team members, customers, as well as the competition.
- Ability to manage time
- Enthusiastic
- Inquisitive
- A great listener
- Ability to quickly interpret, analyze, and respond to information during the sales process
- Ability to connect and develop relationships of trust with potential clients
- Professional appearance

## Team Building – Keeping Your Team Together

In many fitness businesses, sales is a department or a whole team of people who work together to generate leads and convert customers. Effective management of your sales team is a skill every business owner should cultivate.

Teambuilding, recruitment, and training will be discussed in later sections, but take some time to consider the following aspects of managing a sales team:

### Communication

- Are targets and results regularly reviewed?

- Are opportunities for input regularly provided?
- Do sales staff members have a clear understanding of what is expected?
- Do all staff members know daily, weekly, and quarterly targets?

**Performance Management**

- Are sales staff members motivated to reach targets?
- Are sales staff recognized and rewarded once those targets are reached?
- Are there opportunities for skills training and development?
- Do staff members have broad and comprehensive product or industry knowledge?
- Is there opportunity for growth within the company?
- Is performance regularly reviewed?

**Operations**

- Do you have a solid understanding of your sales numbers (revenue, profit, margins)?
- Are your sales processes regularly reviewed?
- Do you have a variety of sales scripts prepared?
- Do you measure conversion rates?
- How are your leads generated?

## Sales Tools

Every salesperson should have an arsenal of tools on hand to assist them in the sales process. These tools can act as aids while a sale is taking place, or help to foster continual learning and development of the salesperson's skills and approach. The list below includes some popular sales tools. Add to this list with other resources that are specific to your business or industry.

| Tool | Description + Benefit |
|---|---|
| **Scripts** | Used for incoming and outgoing telemarketing, cold calls, door-to-door sales, in-store sales.<br>Create several different scripts throughout your business<br>Maintains consistency in your sales approach<br>Revise and renew your scripts regularly |
| **Presentation Materials** | High-quality information about your product or service<br>Forms: PowerPoint presentation, brochure, product sheets, proposal<br>Serves as an outline of your sales presentation, and keeps you on task |
| **Colleagues** | A source of help and advice, especially when you are on the same team or sell similar products<br>Also a source of support |
| **Customer Databases** | An accurate, up-to-date database of customer contact information and contact history<br>Used to stay in touch with clients<br>Can also be used for direct mail and follow-up telemarketing |
| **The Internet** | A powerful resource for sales help and advice<br>Information to help improve your sales process<br>Online sales coaching<br>Source for product knowledge |

| | |
|---|---|
| **Ongoing Training** | Constant improvement of your sales skills<br>Constant increase in product knowledge<br>Investment in yourself and your company |

## 8 Tips for Better Sales

- **Dress for the sale.** Dress professionally, appear well put together and maintain good hygiene. Ensure you are not only dressed professionally, but *appropriately*. Would your client feel more comfortable if you wore a suit, or jeans and blazer?
- **Speak their language.** Show you understand their industry or culture, and use phrases your customer understands. This may require researching industry jargon or common phrases. Remember to avoid using words and phrases that are used in the sales process: sold, contract, telemarketing, finance, interest, etc. Doing so will help break down the salesperson/customer barrier.
- **Ooze positivity**. Show up or answer the phone with a smile, and leave your personal or business issues behind. Be enthusiastic about what you have to offer, and how that offering will benefit your customer. Reflect this not only in your voice, but also in your body language.
- **Deliver a strong pitch or presentation**. Be confident and convincing. Leave self-doubt at the door, and walk in assuming the sale. Take time to explain complex concepts, and always connect what you're saying to your audience in a specific way.
- **Be a poster-child for good manners**. Accept any amenity you're offered, listen intently, don't interrupt, don't show up late, have a

strong handshake, and give everyone you are speaking to equal attention.

- **Avoid sensitive subjects**. Politics, religion, swearing, sexual innuendos and racial comments are absolutely off-limits. So are negative comments about other customers or the competition.
- **Create a real relationship.** Icebreakers and small talk are not just to pass the time before your presentation. They are how relationships get established. Show genuine interest in everything your prospect has to say. Ask questions about topics you know they are passionate about. Speak person to person, not salesperson to customer. Remember everything.
- **Know more than you need to.** Impress clients with comprehensive knowledge – not only of your product or service – but also of the people who use that product or service, and fitness industry trends. Been seen as an expert in order to build trust and respect.

# 5

## Risk Reversal to Increase Sales

What is the biggest objection you need to overcome when closing a sale? Is it cost? Belief in what you have to say? Confidence in your product or service?

While it may be a different answer for different fitness businesses, every fitness business has to deal with some element of customer fear or hesitation before a monetary transaction.

The reality is that even if you overcome these objections and close the sale, your customer walks away carrying 99% of the risk associated with the purchase. If the health clubs fitness services don't perform to expectations, your member has parted with their dollars in exchange for disappointment.

In marketing, your objective is to generate as many leads as possible, then to convert each lead into a customer, or sale. The ratio of leads to closed sales is called your conversion rate.

What if you could eliminate the risk involved in a transaction? Would you turn more leads into members? The answer is absolutely.

Introducing a risk reversal element into your marketing message or unique offer is a powerful way to give yourself an edge on the competition and close more sales. But how exactly are you going to do this?

**It's easy – just give them a guarantee.**

## The Power of Guarantees

### What is Risk Reversal?

Risk reversal simply refers to reversing the risk associated with a transaction – transferring it from the customer to the vendor.

Everyone can think of a handful of times they have purchased a product or service that did not deliver on their expectations. A time where a salesperson made them a promise and did not deliver. A time where they *lost money* on a faulty product or bogus service.

Fear of being burned or taken advantage of prevents many people from spending their money. Customers can also be very wary of buying a product or service for the first time.

Providing a strong guarantee eliminates the majority of risk involved in the purchase, and breaks down natural barriers in the sales process. Guarantees will often shorten the sales process all together – skipping any discussion of objections – because the customer does not see any risk in "trying the product out."

There is also a growing consumer expectation when it comes to guarantees. Many stores will take back anything the customer has not been happy with, and return money or store credit. Popular health food stores encourage customers to try new or unfamiliar products by promising a hassle-free, no questions asked return process. A guarantee or easy return policy can be the difference between choosing one business over its competition.

### Your customers buy results, not products or services

The strongest guarantee you can make is on *results*, not products or services.

If you guarantee that your customer will receive the benefits or results they are looking for, the specific product or service they'll need to achieve those results becomes irrelevant.

People buy benefits and results. For example, they don't buy water purifiers; they buy the benefit enjoying clean, fresh-tasting water. They don't buy lawn sprinkler systems; they buy a healthy green lawn.

Once you understand what specific benefit or solution your customers are seeking, find a way to guarantee they'll receive or experience that solution. If they don't, you'll compensate them for it.

### Remember what you have guaranteed

While guarantees will increase sales for most fitness businesses, they can also be the fast track to business failure if their product or service isn't a quality one. Take the time to ensure you have a strong offering before you implement a guarantee.

Guarantees are most effective when you are selling someone something they need or want – not when you are trying to convince someone to purchase something they have no use for.

## Increasing Conversion Rates with a Guarantee

Guarantees can help your business turn more qualified leads into repeat customers. Strong guarantees are big and bold, but also realistic. They're just a little bit better than your competition, but consistent with the industry's standards.

### Your conversion rate

Your conversion rate is the percentage of prospects you convert from leads into members. The higher your conversion rate, the more revenue you will generate.

To figure out your conversion rate, divide the number of people who purchase from you by the number of people who inquired about your product or service. This will generate a percentage value of your conversion rate.

Guarantees encourage and increase conversion. They motivate potential customers to buy – and to buy from you – because you stand behind what you sell in a big way. There is no risk involved in purchasing what you have to offer.

**Creating your guarantee**

So you're convinced your fitness business – and your members – would benefit from a strong guarantee. Now what? What are you going to guarantee? How are you going to position it?

Once again, this goes back to your target audience and your product or service. What are some of the major objections your potential members raise during the sales process? What kind of risk do they take on when they make a purchase? How much time will they need to test or experience your product or service?

Brainstorm a list of things about your industry that really frustrate your members. They could be service-based (contractors that don't show up, employees who don't perform) or product-based (products that break, do not perform). Then, take a look at your list and decide how you can make sure these things do not happen. Think big – you can do a lot more than you think – then determine if you can actually make good on your promise. If

you can't guarantee the first frustration, then move on to the second.

**Here are some tips on writing your guarantee:**

- **Be specific**. Explain exactly what you are guaranteeing. Don't make vague guarantees that a product will "work" or a service will make you "happy". These words mean different things to different people. Guarantee specific performance or results.

- **Include a clear timeframe.** Put a realistic timeframe on your guarantee. Very few products or services are good forever. Offer a 30-day or 90-day free trial; guarantee results within a set number of days or weeks. This can protect your fitness company, and sets out clear expectations for your clients.
- **Be bold**. Unbelievable guarantees get a customer's attention, so go as far as you realistically can with your claim. Find a way to stand out over the competition – which may also have a guarantee.
- **Tell them what you'll do**. Explain what you'll do – how you'll compensate them – if your product or service doesn't deliver. Be specific, talk money, and go above and beyond.

## Implementing guarantees

### Tell your clients!

Put your guarantee everywhere – your website, brochures, receipt tape, in-store signage, advertisements, and other promotional materials. It will only help attract customers if they know about it.

Send a newsletter to your existing client base informing them of your new guarantees – you never know how many customers you can convince to come back and spend more in your business.

### Train your Staff

Once you have decided to offer your clients a guarantee, you need to ensure your staff are properly trained on the specific policies and procedures associated with that guarantee. If you offer different guarantees for different products and services, ensure this is made clear as well.

Presumably, your staff will be communicating the details of your guarantee, and fielding member questions. They will have to know how to sell the product using the guarantee as a benefit, and understand every application of the guarantee in your business. Every scenario a customer may need to use it.

To ensure your staff is not making any false claims or promises, create a guarantee script for them to use and stick to. This will prevent members from returning with false hopes for their money back, or other compensation.

## Returns + Claims

So, by now you must be thinking, “Great, I can convert more prospects with a strong guarantee, and increase my sales. But what about the added risk I have taken on from my members? Won’t I start to see a ton of returns and service claims?” This is a valid question. Making a strong guarantee means standing by it and delivering on your promise. Inevitably, when you guarantee something, someone is going to take you up on that guarantee and make a claim. I’m going to answer this question in two parts:

**1. Stand behind your product or service.** You’re not in business to scam customers. If you sell a product or service, and you believe in it enough to offer it to your customers, it is likely a quality product or genuine service.

If this is a concern to you, consider implementing strong quality controls or stronger criteria for your merchandising. Companies that offer products and services that deliver results can offer the strongest guarantees.

Of course you will get returns. You will have members come in to take advantage of you. Just remember that as long as the increase in sales outweighs the claims, your guarantee strategy has been successful.

**2. Understand your member's likely behavior.** The truth is that most club members will never take advantage of your guarantee – regardless of their satisfaction level. There are a number of reasons for this.

The first is that most people can't be bothered to drive, mail, or otherwise seek a refund on an item under $50. Many let the timeframe slip by, and have an "oh well" attitude.

The second is that most people don't like confrontation. There is usually an element of confrontation involved in telling someone you didn't like a product or service, and many people do not have the confidence to do so. They'd rather eat the cost than go through the process of asking for a refund.

**Handling claims and returns:**

If you do have your product returned or membership cancelled, it is in your company's best interest to create a system for handling these members interactions.

**Create a claim form**

Ensure that each member who makes a claim about your product or service fills out a standard form. Doing so will help you prevent fraud, gather important information about the member and their reasoning, and create a "hoop" for the customer to jump through if they want their money back.

*Name*

*Date*

*Contact Information*

*Salesperson*

*Product*

*Reason for claim*

*Comments*

*Follow-up*

**Keep a claim or return log**

Create a log or filing system for your claims. This will give you a snapshot of your guarantee program, a record-keeping system, and a wealth of information about each customer's experience and motivations.

**Use the information**

Take the claim forms your customers have filled out, and review them regularly. While some of the claims won't be genuine, there will be some real feedback you can use to improve your product or service, or to modify your guarantee. You may need to make it more realistic, or change the specifics.

# 6

# Creating Effective Marketing Material

Your marketing collateral gets sent out in the world to do one thing: act as an ambassador for your product or service, in place of *you.* This may seem like a big job for a piece of paper, but it's a helpful way to think about the materials you create.

When you meet with a potential or existing client, you do a number of things. You make sure you are well prepared with all the information the customer could need. You dress in clothing that is appropriate. You anticipate their needs, and offer a solution to their problems. You may also cater to how they best like to receive information.

Chances are, you wouldn't meet with clients just for the sake of meeting with a client – say, for instance, to show off your new suit. Likewise, you shouldn't create and distribute collateral that is non-essential.

We all know that the biggest challenge for small businesses is the limited number of zeros attached to their marketing budget. Marketing materials can be expensive, and a single, well-produced piece has the ability to devour the entire budget. Given that billion-dollar marketing campaigns fail every day, how can you be sure to make the most of, and be successful with, the dollars you're working within?

The answer? Limit yourself to only the essential items for your individual business, and produce them *well* with the resources you have.

### Your Essential Marketing Materials

The easiest way to throw away your marketing budget is to create and produce marketing materials *you don't need.* Since many pieces of collateral are paper-based, this not only leaves you with boxes of extra (outdated) materials, but also takes a huge toll on the environment.

Take some time to determine what marketing materials you do need, and stick to your list. It's easy to want to "keep up with the Joneses" when your competition comes out with a new piece, but remember your focus should be on attracting and retaining a customer base, not matching the competition item for item.

**Know your target market.** Make sure you have a solid understanding of your customer base. From that knowledge, you can easily determine what the best way is to reach out and communicate with them. Are they a paper-based or techno savvy client group? Do they appreciate being contacted by email or mail? Are they impressed by flashy design, or simple pieces? *How* you communicate is often just as or more important than *what* you communicate.

**Pay attention to costs.** Do you really need a die-cut business card? Does your flyer absolutely require ink to the edges? Unique touches to marketing collateral can grab a customer's attention, but they can also dramatically increase the cost of production. Keep an eye out during the design process and make strategic choices about graphic elements.

**Make mistakes – in small batches.** Not sure if that flyer is going to do the trick? Testing out a limited time offer? Small production runs may cost a little more, but you'll avoid collecting boxes of unusable materials. Or, try a split run with type versions of the same piece and see what works best.

**Keep the environment in mind.** Environmental responsibility is on everyone's mind these days – including your customers. Always question if a particular marketing item can be produced in electronic format. Consider eliminating plastic bags in exchange for cloth ones, printed with your logo; print everything double-sided; send electronic newsletters; use your website to communicate; and, use recycled paper and envelopes when you can.

**Brainstorm your wish list.** Create a list of desired marketing materials, and ignore expenses, clients, or any other constraint. Then, beside each item, indicate realistically if it is a needed, wanted, not needed, or electronic item. The next page includes a checklist to get you started. Once you have finished, re-write your list in priority order. This will keep you focused on the essentials only.

## Marketing Materials Checklist

| **Item** | **Need** | **Want** | **Don't Need** | **Electronic** |
|---|---|---|---|---|
| Logo | | | | |
| Business Cards | | | | |
| Brochure | | | | |
| Website | | | | |
| Newsletter | | | | |
| Catalogue | | | | |
| Advertisements | | | | |
| Flyers | | | | |
| Fridge Magnet | | | | |
| Branded Swag (pens, etc.) | | | | |
| Employee Clothing | | | | |
| Product Labels | | | | |
| Signage | | | | |
| Internal Templates (Fax Cover, Memo, etc.) | | | | |

| | | | | |
|---|---|---|---|---|
| Email Signature | | | | |
| Blog | | | | |
| Letterhead + Envelopes | | | | |
| Thank You Cards | | | | |
| Notepads | | | | |
| Seasonal Gifts | | | | |
| Company Profile | | | | |

## Headlines + Sub headlines

If your headlines were all a potential customer read, how do you think your marketing materials would fare? Headlines need to be bold, dramatic, shocking and absolutely answer the questions "What's in it for me?" or, "Why should I care?"

Headlines (and sub headlines) are vital in today's market because we are bombarded with so much information that we scan everything. Readers are skimming your materials to find out why they should bother paying attention to your product or service. Hit their hot buttons, and tell them why they should care, in your headlines!

Remember that headlines and sub headlines are not just for advertisements. They work wonders in newsletters, sales letters, brochures and websites, and can be incorporated into all of your essential marketing materials.

## Design

The cost of professional design can eat up the majority of your marketing budget in a hurry. However, the cost of distributing materials that look and feel unprofessional can often be much higher. The key is to find the middle ground.

Unless you have design or desktop publishing experience – or even if you do – your time is probably not best spent designing your own marketing materials. Depending on the size of your business and your graphic needs (i.e., Do you need frequent photography of your products?) there are a number of options you can choose from:

1. **Hire a design agency.** This is no doubt the most costly of your options. However, if you have a number of items to be designed, you may be able to get a package rate. Another option is to have the design agency create a logo and stationery package for you, then create a "how-to" guide for use of the logo, fonts, and other graphic elements in the rest of your marketing materials.
2. **Hire a freelance designer.** For most small businesses, the benefits of using a freelance designer (aside from cost savings) are convenience and trust. If you are lucky enough to find one you work well with, work hard to establish a seamless working relationship and you'll never worry about the design of your marketing materials again. Ask colleagues for recommendations of local designers, or post an ad on craigslist.
3. **Hire a part-time design employee.** Need to hire someone part-time for a task around the office or shop? Consider recruiting someone with design skills and hiring them for full-time work. This could include graphic design students, or someone with an interest (and talent) in the field.

Whichever option you choose – or if you choose to design your materials yourself - the two most important things to remember about design are:

1. **Keep it consistent.** Your marketing materials must be consistent, or your customers will never learn to recognize your brand.

2. **Keep it simple.** Simple, clean design is the most effective way of communicating. Use "wow" pieces sparingly.

## Guidelines for the Top 10 Marketing Materials

### Logo

- **Use design resources.** If you are going to spend any money on outside design help, this is the time to do it. Your logo is the visual representation of your fitness product or service, and appears on everything that relates to your business. This is the core of your brand image, and needs to be done right the first time.
- **Remember the purpose.** The logo needs to be a unique reflection of your fitness business, your fitness business values, and the industry you work in. Before you commit to your logo, make sure to give careful consideration to color choice, image selection and image recognition – as well as the logos that already exist in the marketplace. Test it out on your family and friends for an outside opinion and use their feedback.
- **Don't get too complicated.** Can it be produced (and seen clearly) in black and white? In a single color? With your company name? Too often fitness businesses design their own logos that include a complex assortment of photos, words, and solid design elements. These do not photocopy well, and can't be clearly read at a small scale. Keep your logo design down to a graphic image and the name of your business.

**Business cards**

- **Cover the basics.** A business card needs to communicate your basic contact information to potential clients, including who you are and *what your business does*. Make sure you've covered the basics and made it easy for them to be in touch.
    - **Name**
    - **Title**
    - **Company Name**
    - **Company Slogan / Description**
    - **Phone Number**
    - **Email Address**
    - **Fax Number**
    - **Address**
    - **Cell Number (if applicable)**
    - **Website**
- **Make it memorable. Be creative.** Choose interesting shapes, die- cuts, orientation (vertical vs. horizontal), bright colors, and unique materials (wood, plastic, magnet, aluminum or foam). You don't have to go crazy or spend lots of money to do this – simple, clever twists on basic design make an impact. Just keep it relevant to your product or service.
- **Give them a reason to keep it.** What is going to keep them from throwing it out, or filing it in a 3" binder of other cards? Make the card worth keeping by adding something useful to the

backside. For example, coffee shops put frequent buyer incentives on the backside of their cards, encouraging customers to keep them in their wallets. Other examples include pick-up schedules, reminders, calendars, testimonials, or coupons.

- **Produce a high quality card.** Use at least 100lb card stock, and print in color. Choose clear, easy to read fonts that aren't any smaller than 9pt.

**Letterhead**

- **Ensure a professional quality.** Letterhead that is simple, clean, and well produced allows the reader to focus on the important part: the content. Have your letterhead professionally printed on 32lb paper, or choose a textured stock. Show that you are invested in the professionalism of your company.
- **Pay attention to design choices.** The design of your marketing collateral should reflect your corporate values and the personality of your organization. If you are environmentally conscious, choose recycled paper and write it in small print at the bottom of the page. Letterhead can also be a place for subtle graphic elements, like watermarks, in addition to your logo.
- **Keep consistent with other materials.** Your letterhead is part of your stationery package, and should look and feel the same as the rest of your pieces. For example, if your business cards have been printed with rounded corners, so should your letterhead. Use consistent fonts, colors, and logo placement on your letterhead, business cards, fax cover sheets, and other internal documents to ensure recognition and ease of readability.

**Brochures**

- **Cover the basics.** Each brochure you produce should include your basic marketing message, USP, and detailed company contact information. Product or service features, and customer benefits should be clearly displayed and described.
- **Be purpose-focused.** Why are you producing this brochure? Are you featuring a new product line? Trying to increase awareness? Introducing your service to a new market? Stay closely connected to the purpose behind your brochure, and ensure that all of the information (and images) in the brochure support that purpose.
- **Keep it simple.** Make sure the design and information organization is clean and easy to navigate. Like advertisements, leaving blank spaces gives the reader a break and makes it easier to narrow in on key messages.
- **Choose high quality production.** If you don't invest in your business, why should anyone else? Produce your brochure on high quality paper, in vivid color, and have it professionally folded. An impressive-looking brochure will travel farther than a homemade one – from one client's hands to another's.
- **Keep it fresh.** If you produce brochures on a regular basis, consider giving each a theme to distinguish the information as new and interesting. Keep the overall look and feel consistent, but play with images and content layout to revitalize the design.

**Newsletters**

- **Be in touch.** Don't wait until your existing clients walk back into your club. Show them they're important to your business, and keep them updated on new products and services by keeping distributing a personalized newsletter.

- **Use an online distribution service.** Online email marketing tools (CRM tools) have never been easier or cheaper to use, and enable you to personalize your letters without much effort. They will also track for you which clients open their newsletters, and which click through to your website.
- **Provide information, tell a story.** Engage the reader with a short anecdote, or a piece of relevant information. Many people are bombarded by hard-copy and electronic letters on a daily basis, so make sure yours is worthy of their reading time. Include an "experts corner" or "new product feature" and structure the newsletter like your own business newspaper. Add links to relevant media articles, or special offers.
- **Choose a frequency you can maintain.** Newsletters can be time consuming, so be realistic about how often you promise to distribute them. This depends on your resources, and the needs of your business, but generally once a month to once every three months is a good time frame.

**Company (or Corporate) Profile**

- **Your ultimate company brochure.** Your company profile includes all pertinent information on your fitness business and your offering, and acts as the base for all other marketing items. These are generally longer pieces – from five to 20 pages in length, allowing you ample room for written and visual content.
- **Tell your story.** The fitness company profile is the place to tell the story of your business. Engage the reader, use anecdotes, and

describe how and why your company was created. If you inherited the family business, describe how you're carrying on tradition and instilling new life. If you created your company from scratch with your college roommate, let the reader know. These real life details are interesting and establish trust with your potential clients and associates.

- **Communicate your values.** Here you have the space to describe your company's vision, values and approach, or philosophies. Make sure you relate your values to your offering, and keep this section short and succinct.
- **Explain your offering – features, benefits and all.** Just like your brochure, make sure to describe the full features and benefits of your product or service. Sprinkle testimonials throughout the design to back up your statements. This can include your full range of services, or simply an overview of your product types. Use professional images and creative copy to keep readers engaged.
- **Choose high-quality design and production.** Spend time creating a company profile that will last. Then, spend money producing one that will impress. Choose glossy paper, and a high-quality press, and leave the profiles around your store and office for clients to read and admire.

**Signage**

- **Get professional advice.** Outdoor signage can be a daunting task for anyone who hasn't designed, produced, or otherwise gone through the process. Since signage is influenced by a variety of factors – one of which is your municipal government signage by law – you may wish to enlist the help of a professional (a signage designer or printer) to guide you through the process and avoid costly errors.

- **Make it visible.** All of your outdoor signage should be easily seen from the street, or within the plaza or complex you are located in. In some cases, you may need more than one sign to do this. Keep in mind how your sign will look at night, as well as during the day, as your company logo and phone number or website needs to be visible at all times.
- **Make it distinct.** When it comes to signage, you can get really creative with materials, lights, and colors. While you need to maintain logo, color, and font consistency, you can add other graphic elements that may not work on the rest of your collateral, including 3D elements and window treatments. Make it memorable.
- **Remember your indoor signage.** Every business needs indoor signage to continually remind customers where they are. This includes section signage, product signage, way finding systems, and promotion announcements. If your fitness business is located in an office, consider signage with your logo and company name above the reception area. Again, keep this signage consistent with the rest of your company materials, and you will be contributing to brand recognition.

**Advertisements + Flyers**

- **Place ads strategically.** Once you have determined who your target market is, you need to focus on advertising in the publications they are most likely to read, and distributing flyers in places they are most likely to be. Spend ad dollars strategically, and don't spend them all at once. Take time to test what publications work, and which don't by measuring the response from each placement. And, when you place ads, request placement that is well-forward and in the top right hand corner.

- **Grab their attention.** You have less than half a second to grab the attention of your audience with print advertising, so use it wisely. Spend the bulk of your time crafting the headline and choosing compelling images.
- **Keep their attention.** If you caught their attention, you have another two seconds to keep it. Use subheadings to further entice them to read on for the details of your product or service offer.
- **Tell them why they should buy.** Always include your marketing message or USP in your advertising. Describe the features and benefits of your product or service, but focus on the benefits that will trigger an emotional response from your target audience – love, money, luxury, convenience, and security.
- **Tell them how they can buy.** Include a call to action beside your contact information, and include your phone number, website address, and business address (if applicable). You may wish to include a scarcity or urgency offer to compel your readers to act fast.
- **Know the importance of white space.** If you try to cram too much information into your ad or flyer, your readers will skip it. Clean, clear, easy to read ads and one-page flyers with succinct messages are most effective.

**Website**

- **Be purpose-focused.** Like your brochure, your website can serve a number of purposes. To be effective, you need to narrow in on the specific purpose when designing the content structure of the pages. Who is your audience? What do you want them to leave the site knowing? What do you want the site to make them do? Visit your store? Buy your offering? Pick up the phone? Make sure you are clear on this point before you start.
- **Make the address easy to remember (and find!).** A website address that is too long or too complicated will not get remembered, or found. Do a search for available website addresses that relate to your business or marketing message, and try to secure a site with a .com ending. If your company name is taken, use your USP or guarantee instead.
- **Focus on content.** The overall structure of how you organize the content on your site is like the foundation of your house. You can change the paint color, and the furniture, but the foundation is more or less there for good. Before you work with a designer and create the visual fabric of your website, focus on creating solid copy that is clearly organized. Put together a map of your structure, starting with your homepage and subpages, and allocating specific content to each page.
- **Revitalize regularly.** Your company is always changing, and so should your website. This is an important (and relatively inexpensive) way to communicate your company news and achievements, and most likely the easiest accessed source of information. Have areas for easy content updates – like a "news" section – and make sure sections like "employees" and

"services" are kept up to date. For larger updates, go back to your purpose and website map, and make sure the content changes still support the original intent of the website.

- **Organize for intuition.** Make key information easy to access – especially your contact information. You can quickly tell if a website is easy to navigate, because the information you are looking for appears in a natural order. For example, when visiting a restaurant website, a link to the reservations page is provided on the menu page. While you're putting together your website map, do some research online and investigate what does and doesn't work. A good rule of thumb is to ensure it takes no more than three clicks to access a page. Bury content too deep, and your audience will get frustrated and leave.

- **Keep consistent with marketing materials.** Your website is an extension of your marketing campaign, and should be treated as such. Use consistent logo placements, fonts, colors and images so that all elements of your collateral are unified. Likewise, with marketing campaigns. If you are running a new promotion, or featuring a new item in an advertisement, include that information on your website. Customers responding to the ad will be reinforced, and customers who did not see the ad will be aware of the offer.

- **Measure your results.** Your website is a piece of your marketing collateral, just like brochures and advertisements, and should be evaluated for effectiveness on a regular basis. Easy website analysis tools, like Google Analytics, will show you which pages your audience is viewing, how long they're staying on each page, and where and when they leave the site. That is powerful information when it comes to structuring content, and choosing which page to put your most important messages.

# 7

# How to Use Advertising for Immediate Profits

Why do you advertise?

Seems like a silly question, doesn't it? Placing ads in newspapers and on the radio seems like a no-brainer way of growing or maintaining your fitness business. You let a group of people know where your business is and what you sell, and you'll always have customers dropping by, right?

Sure, it's a little more complicated than that. There's your powerful offer, your strong guarantee, the placement of your headline, and how you structure your body copy.

But what I'm really trying to drill down to is *why* you chose to place *that* ad. What is the specific purpose for each advertisement you send out into the world?

Without a solid purpose – or strategy – behind each and every advertisement, it is impossible to measure what is and is not working. If you placed an ad offering 2 for 1 shampoo one week, and sales for conditioner skyrocketed, would you consider your ad successful? Absolutely not. Sales might have gone up, but the reason you placed the ad was to speed sales on shampoo, which didn't happen. The point is that each and every advertising dollar should be spent with purpose, focused on a desired outcome and relevant to the big picture. Advertising is expensive! What's the point, unless you're making your money back and then some?

## Types of Advertising

There are endless options when it comes to choosing which media to place your advertisements with. The media is a broad and complicated industry, with highly segmented readership.

This can help and hurt your advertising efforts. You have access to highly targeted audiences, but you also may spend a great deal of money on expensive advertising that your target market doesn't go near.

Here are the major types of media advertising:

### Print

Print is the most common form of advertising. Ad production is relatively easy and straightforward, and placement is less expensive than broadcast advertising. We'll be focusing on this form of advertising in detail later in the chapter.

**Types of print media:**

Newspapers – daily and weekly

Magazines

Trade Journals

Newsletters

### Radio

Radio advertising reaches a broad audience within a geographic area. This form of advertising can be highly profitable for some businesses, and utterly useless for others. Always consider if there is a simpler, cheaper way of getting your message to your target audience.

**Key points to consider for radio advertising:**

Use of sounds, voices, tones

Length

Gaining listener's attention

Call to action

**Television**

Television advertising is largely out of reach for most small business budgets. Creating, developing, and producing TV spots is a costly endeavor, and does not always generate an acceptable return on investment.

This form of advertising generally reaches a broad audience, depending on the timeslot the ad spot airs. Typically, the most expensive airspace is during the region's most popular 6 o'clock news program, or prime time (6pm to 10pm) television line-up.

There are some cost-effective alternatives to TV advertising that you can implement online. You could create a promotional video for your fitness company, and post it on your website and YouTube, or Facebook, or play it in your store. Be creative with your ad budget when it comes to broadcast media.

**Online**

Online advertising has emerged as an effective tool for your marketing efforts. Internet usage has dramatically increased, and usage patterns have become easier to identify. This form of advertising also allows you to reach a highly qualified audience with minimal investment in ad creation.

**Places to advertise online:**

Facebook

Google AdWords

Online media (online newspapers and broadcast stations)

Craigslist

Banner ads on complementary websites

**Classified**

Classified advertising is one of the most highly targeted and cost-effective choices you can make in your overall strategy. People who read classifieds have typically made a decision to buy something, and are looking for places to do so. This is also a great way to test your headlines, offer, and guarantee before you invest in higher-priced advertising.

**Classified ad types:**

Daily and weekly newspapers

Online

Trade journals

**Specific tips for effective classified ads:**

- Pick a format for your ad within the specifications of the publication. Will it look like a print display ad? A semi-display ad? A classic line ad? This will affect how you structure your message.
- Choose the category – or two – that best fit with what you have to offer. If two apply, place an ad in both and measure which category generated more leads.
- Grab the attention of your reader with a killer headline, then list benefits, make an irresistible offer, and offer a strong guarantee. Keep the layout simple and ensure the font size is easy to read.
- Notice how other companies are creating their ads, and do something to stand out. The classifieds page is typically cluttered

and full of text, so you will need to distinguish your business in some way.

- Use standard abbreviations when creating line ads to maintain consistency. Ask the ad department for a list of abbreviations they typically use.

**Niche**

Niche advertising can take any of the forms discussed above. The advantage of niche advertising is the super segmentation of each outlet's audience. Typically, there is a very small market in each niche, and a single publication that caters to it. This is very effective for fitness companies who have no need for broad market advertising in traditional or mainstream publications.

**Types of niche advertising:**

Trade journals

Alternative media

Online blogs

Internal communications – newsletters, etc.

## Your Advertising Strategy

**Develop a strategy that is purpose driven.**

Know exactly why you are choosing advertising, as well as the objective of each and every ad. Compare the benefits of advertising to other promotional strategies like media relations, direct mail, referral strategies and customer loyalty programs.

Some common objectives for advertising strategies include:

- Generate qualified leads
- Increase sales
- Promote new products or services
- Position products or services
- Increase business awareness
- Maintain business awareness
- Complement existing promotional strategies

These objectives will dictate where you advertise, how big each of your advertisements is, and how often you advertise in each outlet.

**Find your target audience.**

Before you do anything, get a solid handle on who your target market is, and each of the segments within it. Think about demographic factors like age, sex, location and occupation, as well as behavioral factors like spending motivations and habits.

The composition of your target audience will be the deciding factor when choosing which media to advertise with, and what to say in each of the advertisements.

**Decide on a frequency.**

The frequency of your advertising campaign will depend on a number of factors, including budget, purpose, outlet, results, and timing. You may wish to publish a weekly ad that includes a coupon in your local paper. Or, you may only need to advertise a few times a year, just before your peak seasons.

Establish an advertising schedule for the year, or at least each quarter, and plan each advertisement in advance. This will ensure you are not scrambling to place an ad at the last minute, and that each ad is part of an overall proactive strategy instead of a reactive one.

**Choose your outlets.**

Decide where you are going to advertise and how often in each outlet. You may wish to choose a variety of media to reach several target audiences, or just a large daily newspaper where the most number of people will see it.

It is a good idea when you are starting a new campaign to test its effectiveness in smaller, less expensive publications. Based on the results, you can make changes to the ad and place it in the more expensive outlets.

**Remember that although budget is a large factor when deciding on advertising mediums, it is entirely possible to implement a successful ad campaign with minimal cost investment. The key is to make sure that each dollar you spend is carefully thought through – and that your ads are placed in publications that will reach your ideal customers.**

**Maximize your ad spend with bulk purchases.**

If you plan to advertise in a specific publication several times in a given time period, you will benefit from a meeting with the sales representative to review your needs. Often, media outlets will offer discounted rates for multiple placements.

Remember that one company may own several media outlets – including TV, radio, and online media. Ask your sales rep for other discount opportunities when advertising within the ownership group.

**Remember to test and measure**

How will you know if your campaign is successful if you don't test and measure the results? The only true mistake you can make in advertising is neglecting to track and analyze the results each ad generates.

Get in the habit of keeping a copy of each ad, and record all the details of the placement, including publication, cost, date, response rate, and conversion rate. Many publications will mail you a clipping of your advertisement with your account statement, but don't rely on this as a clipping service.

Evaluate the effectiveness of each ad you place, and learn from what isn't working. If you are advertising in several outlets, make sure asking customers where they saw your ad is part of your incoming phone script and sales script. You will need to monitor not only what types of ads work the best, but also where the ads generate the highest response.

## Creating Your Advertisement

You don't need to rely on professional copywriting or design assistance when crafting advertisements from your business. Spend your time and resources on what you are saying, ensure the 'how you say it' is clear, clean, and easy to read.

**Ad copy**

**Headlines**

- Take at least half of the time you spend creating your ad, and focus on the headline. Your headline will be the difference between your ad getting read – or not. Boldface your headlines for impact.
- You have about five seconds to grab the reader's attention, so create a headline that sparks curiosity, communicates benefits, or states something unbelievable.

**Sub Headlines**

- The purpose of your sub headline is to elaborate on your headline, and convince the audience to read the body copy. All the rules of headline writing apply. If you did not mention benefits in your headline, do it in your sub headline. Clearly tell the reader what is "in it for them," and get them reading on.

**Body Copy**

- Choose your words wisely – you don't have room for lengthy paragraphs. Use bullet points to convey benefits wherever possible, and keep your sentences short. You typically only have about 45 words to convince the customer to keep reading.
- Remember to always include your contact information – phone number and website address at the very least. This seems obvious, but can be forgotten in the design process.

**Ad Layout**

**Size**

- Choose your ad size based on the purpose of the ad, and the budget you have available. Larger ads are more expensive, but you do need enough space to communicate your key messages to the audience.
- If you place regular ads to maintain a presence in the local paper, you likely don't need full pages of space. Alternately, if you are launching a new product or service, or having a blowout sale, you will want to buy more space to increase the potential impact.

**Graphics**

- Graphics should comprise about 25% of your total ad space, and more if you have a small amount of copy. Avoid drawings and clip art. Photographs will generate a better response. Don't underestimate the importance of white space. Give the reader space to “rest” their eyes between headlines and body copy paragraphs.

**Font**

- Choose clean fonts that are easy to read. Times New Roman and Arial are effective, simple choices. If you use two fonts in your advertisement, make sure you do not combine serif and sans serif fonts, and you keep consistency amongst headers and body copy.
- Ensure that none of your copy is smaller than 9pt. Your audience won’t take the time or spend the effort to read tiny copy.

# 8

# How to Create Repeat Business and Have Members that Pay, Stay and Refer

When it comes to marketing and generating more income, most fitness business owners are focused outward.

They've carefully established and segmented their target market, and created specific offers and messages for each market segment. They spend thousands of dollars in advertising and direct mail campaigns in hot pursuit of more leads, more customers, and more foot traffic.

While this is an effective way to build a business, it is costly and time consuming. It requires constant and consistent effort, and while this approach does generate results, those results quickly disappear when the effort stops or becomes less intense.

Successful fitness businesses that see sustained growth have a double-edged marketing strategy. They focus their efforts *outward* – on new potential customers and marketing – as well as *inward* – on existing customers and referral business.

These successful businesses have leveraged their existing efforts to generate more revenue. Simply put, their customers buy from them over and over again.

For most fitness businesses, this is the easiest way to increase their revenues. Simple customer loyalty strategies and outstanding customer service are often all you need to dramatically increase your sales – from the customers you already have.

## The Cost of Your Members

Do you know how much it costs your fitness business to buy new customers?

Each new customer that walks through your door – with the exception of referrals – has cost you money to acquire. You have spent money on advertising and promotions to generate leads and turn those leads into customers.

For example, if you have placed an ad in your local newspaper for $1,000, and the ad brings in 10 customers, you have paid $100 to acquire each customer. You would need to ensure each of those customers spent at least $200 to cover your margin and break even.

Alternately, if you spent two hours of your time and $10 per month on an email marketing program to send a newsletter to your existing database of customers, and you bring in 10 customers as a result – each customer has cost you $1.

Generating more repeat business means focusing on the marketing strategies that aim to keep your existing members instead of purchase new ones – effectively reducing the cost of attracting new members to your health club.

These strategies are simple to implement, and don't require much time investment. Just a solid understanding of how to make customers want to come back and spend more of their money.

## Keeping Your Members

Marketing strategies that focus on keeping your current member base are easy and enjoyable to implement. They allow you to build real relationships with the people you do business with, instead of dealing with a revolving door of people on the other end of your sales process.

Repeat customers create a community of people around your business that presumably share the same needs, desires and frustrations. The information you gain from these customers (market research) can help you strengthen your understanding of your target audience, and more accurately segment it.

Remember – 80% of your revenue comes from 20% of your members. Always focus on these members. They are ideal members that you want to recruit, and hold on to.

**Customer Service: Make them love buying from you**

Every business – even those with excellent service standards can improve the service they provide their customers. Customer service seems to be a dying concept in most businesses; more focus seems to be placed on the speed of the transaction. These days you can even go to the grocery store now and not speak to a single sales associate thanks to self-serve checkouts.

To improve your company's customer service standards, take a survey of your customers and your employees to brainstorm ways you can improve the experience of buying from your fitness business.

Successful customer service standards – those that make your customers *buy* – are:

**Consistent**. The standards are up kept by every person in your organization. Expectations are clear and followed through. Customers know what to expect, and choose your business because of those expectations.

**Convenient**. It is nearly effortless for the customer to spend money at your place of business. Convenience can take many forms – location, product selection, value-added services like delivery – and it is also consistent.

**Customer-driven**. The service the customer receives is exactly how they would like to be treated when buying your product or service. It is reflective of your target market, and appropriate to their lifestyle. Customers would probably not appreciate white linen tablecloths at a fast food restaurant, but they would appreciate a 2-minutes or less guarantee.

**Newsletters: Keep in touch with your customers**

A regular newsletter is an easy, time-effective, and inexpensive marketing strategy to implement. Unfortunately, many small businesses think these are too time consuming and too expensive to adopt as part of their marketing strategy.

The most popular type of newsletter distribution is email. This will cost your business as little at $10 per month for an email marketing service subscription, and can be customized to your unique branding.

Here is an easy five-step process to starting a company newsletter:

1. **Pick your audience.** New customers? Market segment? Existing customers?
2. **Choose what you're going to say.** Company news? Feature product? New offer?
3. **Determine how you're going to say it.** Articles? Bullet points? Pictures?
4. **Decide how it's going to get to your audience.** Email? Mail? In-store?
5. **Track your results.** How many people opened it? Read it? Took action?

**Value Added Service: Give them happy surprises**

Adding value to your business is an effective way of getting your customers back. Every person I know would choose a mattress store that offered free delivery over one that did not. It's that simple.

There are many ways to add value to your business, including:

- **Feature your expertise.** Use your knowledge to provide additional value to your customers. Offer a free consumer guide or report with every purchase.
- **Add convenience services.** Offer a service that makes their purchase easier, or more convenient. The best example of this is free shipping or delivery.
- **Package complementary services**. Packaging like items together creates an increase in perceived value. This is great for start-up kits.
- **Offer new products or services**. Feature top of the line or exclusive products, available only at your health club. Offer a new service or profile a new staff member with niche expertise.

Value added services generate repeat customers in one of two ways:

**1. Impress them on their first visit.** Impress your members with great service, a product that meets their needs, and then wow them with something extra that they weren't expecting. Get them to associate the experience of dealing with your business with happy surprises, and create a perception of higher value.

**2. Entice them to come back.** The introduction of a new value- added service can be enough to convince a member to buy from you again. Their initial purchase established a trust and knowledge of your business and its processes. They will want to "be included" in anything new you have to offer – especially if there is exclusivity. It is easier to attract clients that have purchased from you than potential clients who have not.

**Customer Loyalty Programs: Give them incentives**

Another simple way to keep in touch with existing customers and keep them coming back to you is to create a customer loyalty program.

These programs do not have to be complicated or costly, and are relatively easy to maintain once they have been implemented. These programs help you gain more information on your members and their purchasing habits.

Here are some examples of simple loyalty programs that you can implement:

**Free product or service.** Give them every 10th (or 6th) product or service free. Produce stamp cards with your logo and contact information on it.

**Reward dollars.** Give them a certain percentage of their purchase back in money that can only be spent in-store. Produce "funny money" with your logo and brand.

**Rewards points.** Give them a certain number of points for every dollar they spend. These points can be spent in-store, or on special items you bring in for points only.

**Membership amenities.** Give members access to VIP amenities that are not available to other members. Produce member cards or give out member numbers.

Remember that in order for this strategy to work, you and your team have to understand and promote it. The program in itself becomes a product that you sell.

# 9

# Create Added Value in Your Fitness Business and Make 1 + 1 = 3

The majority of fitness businesses, like yours, are established in response to market demand for a product or service. Many build their businesses by serving that demand, and enjoy growing profits without putting much effort into long-term planning or marketing.

However, what happens when that demand slows or stops? What happens when the competition sets up shop with a "new and improved" version of your product down the road? How do you keep your offering fresh, while growing and maintaining your member base? The answer is by adding value to your product or service.

Added value is a marketing or customer relations strategy that can take the form of a product, service, which is added to the original offering for free, or as part of a discounted package. It, like all other elements in your marketing toolkit, is designed to attract new customers and retain existing ones. A simple example of added value would be if you owned a gift shop, and offered complimentary gift wrapping with every purchase.

If you don't refresh and renew your offering over time, your members will get bored and be drawn to your competitor. Your employees, too, may become disinterested, and find work elsewhere. Ultimately, both clients and employees will demand additional value to remain loyal – and aren't they the keystones for your business growth?

## Can You Add Value to Your Fitness Business?

Everyone can add value to their fitness business. Better yet, everyone can *afford* to add value to their business. Adding value doesn't have to blow your marketing budget, or take up hours of your time. There are many ways – big and small – to enhance your business in the eyes of your members.

The key to adding value is determining what your members and target market perceive as valuable. You must understand their needs, wants, troubles and inconveniences in order to entice them with solutions through added value products or services. Adding value will add to your profits, but if you don't focus on genuinely helping your clients, you'll have a difficult time attracting them.

Added value works for both product- and service-based businesses. If you offer a service, like hairstyling, try treating your customers with products like a latte while they wait, shampoo samples, or a free conditioning treatment with every sixth visit. If you sell a product, consider offering convenience services – like free auto-shipping or delivery – to make the customer's experience a seamless one. The customer will feel appreciated and their needs will have been taken care of.

## Ways to Add Value to Your Fitness Business

There are many ways to enhance your offer, depending on your budget and the resources you have access to. You may wish to hold a brainstorming session with your staff to come up with ideas for your business; if your employees are on the front lines, they'll likely have firsthand information about what clients would like to see more of.

### Feature Your Expertise

Your intellectual property is a free resource that you have at your disposal to share with your members. This will make them feel as though they have an inside track. You might want to consider adding it to your business, making it a value-added service.

**Expert corner:** Supplement your website and newsletter with columns on topics of interest to your customers and of relevance to your service. This will position you as an expert in the marketplace, and give your clients helpful information they won't receive from the competition.

**Do It Yourself Tips:** This is a great tool for seasonal marketing. Provide your clients with this information on your website, in your newsletters, or on take one free passes in your club or office. Ideas include recipes, craft ideas, gift ideas – all of which are branded with your company logo and contact information, and include your product as an ingredient.

**What to Expect Tips:** Take your customer through what they should expect in the first few days (weeks) of using your service or product,

and how they can make the most of it.

**Related + Community Events:** Own a store that sells athletic equipment? Post information on your website, in store, and in your newsletter about upcoming races, games, or consumer trade shows. Or simply keep a bulletin in your office of community events and offers that will draw your members in, and establish itself as a hub in the neighborhood for information.

**Offer Convenience Services**

Customer service is a dying practice in our high paced culture – use it to your advantage. When done well, it can be the difference between you and the competition, or the deciding factor for a potential repeat client.

Envision the steps involved for a member to arrive at your club, purchase your offering, and use your product or service. Can you eliminate any of those steps for them? Can you shorten waiting times, or make them more pleasurable? Stepping into your clients' shoes will allow you to determine the most powerful value add for your fitness company. Here are a few ideas:

**Free Delivery + Shipping:** With clearly established parameters (will you ship your product free to India?), this is a solid value added service that many businesses offer. Free delivery (usually with a purchase over a set amount) is a huge convenience for many people who do not have access to a vehicle, or need help moving large items.

**Follow up Services:** This works great for salespeople, trainers, and customer service representatives, members will rely on you for assistance which brings them back into the club and establishes a relationship of trust.

**Gift-Certificates:** A great service to provide – especially for seasonal gifts. Gift Certificates cost very little, and can have a big impact on your business.

**"While You Wait" Amenities:** If you could make your customer feel like a VIP for minimal cost, why wouldn't you? Offering amenities like coffee and treats, free samples and services (wireless internet is a big one) will go a long way.

**Comparison-Shopping Tools:** Show your prospects that you are so sure your product will measure up against the competition, that you'll help them compare.

### Establish Complementary Partnerships

Complementary partnerships with other businesses can take you a long way toward adding value for your customer, and generating new business. Just like a joint testimonial mailing, the power (and convenience) of referral business is immense.

**Build a web of associates:** If you're a yoga instructor, carry the cards of your treatment providers (physiotherapists, massage therapists, etc.) to refer your students to. In exchange, your brochure or card is posted in their offices. This works for automotive repair, esthetics, consultants and other service providers. Customers will trust referrals received by their existing service providers, and feel taken care of by a reputable community of experts.

**Establish partnerships with financial incentives:** This is one that has your interests in mind as well as your customers'. In addition to establishing a complementary partnership with a related associate, establish an incentive structure where each of you are compensated for your referrals. For example, if you refer a client to a furniture store after they've purchased a mattress from you, and they buy a bed frame, your associate will pay you a portion of the sale – and vice versa.

**Location-based partnerships:** Consider creating partnerships with the businesses around you – even if your products and services don't appear to be related. Shopping malls do this all the time with value coupon books that customers must purchase for $5 to $20 dollars. These partnerships and incentives will keep the customer spending money in the area, which is good for everyone's bottom line.

**Packages + Bundles**

Packaging and bundling products and services is one of the most popular methods of adding value. Members perceive the bundles as having a higher value than the sum of the individual items – or as receiving something for free.

Cleverly packaged and named bundles can spark interest and revive your products in the eyes of your customers. Remember to always give the offers an end date or provide a limited number to create a sense of scarcity and urgency and to prevent this strategy from going stale.

**Intuitive product bundles:** Package independent related products together, and give them a reduced price or name. For example, this could be selling an extra pair of running socks with new running shoes. Remember the convenience of starter kits – package everything your customer will need to begin a new activity – painting, camping, running, etc. – in a bundle for simple buying decisions.

**Package your upsell**: This can also be called a chain of purchasing. It includes the products or services your client will need to use your product or service. Won't they need gloves and/or wraps for their boxing class? By packaging these clearly related products together, you are making their shopping experience faster and more convenient.

**Offer a Customer Loyalty Program**

There are a number of ways to structure your rewards and loyalty program, depending on the type of business and level of technological resources available to you. Customer loyalty programs have a huge advantage – they help build your database of member information and in most cases allow you to view and analyze purchasing patterns. Here are the most popular:

**Every 6th (or 10th) Visit on Us:** This works well for business that rely on repeat visits from their members – like private fitness studios and health clubs, etc. Customers receive a card with store information on the front, and space for stamps or initials on the back. Remember that while 10 is a nice even number, it may be too far in the future for some customers (especially for services that are three to six weeks apart). The idea of six visits is more manageable.

**Rewards Dollars:** This is the Canadian Tire model. For every dollar your customer spends in store, they receive a small portion back in store credit (i.e., Canadian Tire money). The store credit is in the form of printed dollars, branded with your company logo and contact information, and serves as a reminder each time a client opens their wallet.

**Rewards Points:** Another common value-add strategy is a rewards points system. Most grocery stores use this incentive, as well as credit card companies. This works the same as rewards dollars, where a certain number of points are accumulated based on each dollar spent in store. Points can then be spent in store, or on products you have brought in for "rewards points holders" only. This strategy also allows you to feature products with "extra points value" instead of discounting prices.

**Membership Amenities:** Instead of points or dollars, you can offer VIP treatment for members, when they sign up for or purchase a membership. This may include occasional discounts, but is primarily centered around perks like "while you wait" amenities, skipping the line, free services, etc. You can also produce membership cards.

# 10

# Profits and Leads through Host Beneficiary Relationships

Did you know that a business just down the street from yours may be able to help double your profits this year? Or does this sound a little too far-fetched?

Maybe. If you operate a retail store that sells tires, and the business down the road is a hair salon, you may have a hard time making this happen. However, loose partnerships between complementary, non-competing businesses can be a financial goldmine when implemented strategically. And your partner may be just steps away!

Formally called Host Beneficiary Relationships, these partnerships help small and medium-sized businesses tap into very specific target markets and close sales under existing relationships of trust.

HB Relationships allow one business (the 'host') to add value to their product or service, and the other (the 'beneficiary') to benefit from the impact of a referral. The beauty of this arrangement is that the roles can then be swapped; the 'host' becomes the 'beneficiary' and vice versa.

Like any marketing strategy, HB Relationships don't work for every business all the time. However, they are a great tool to keep in your marketing arsenal when starting a business, entering new markets, boosting product sales, or any other opportunity that requires a specific and personal approach.

## How Can a HB Relationship Help Your Fitness Business?

Establishing, planning, and implementing a successful HB Relationship campaign is more complex than asking your neighbor to send a letter to his client base with an offer from your company.

As with every other component of your marketing strategy and materials, an HB Relationship campaign must be purpose-driven and evaluated to be the best approach to secure your desired results.

For example, if your business caters to a broad audience and you have an irresistible offer that is going to have people running through your doors, you may want to consider a simple advertisement that will reach the most people. Alternately, if you offer a common product with a low price point – like coffee or candy – it's unlikely that a HB Relationship is worth the cost and effort involved.

So in what cases will a Host Beneficiary Relationship benefit your business?

**1. A Start-up Company**

A company that is just starting out has the most to gain from a HB Relationship. Faced with the standard challenges of establishing a new operation – credibility, product positioning, target market establishment, marketing strategy, etc. – a HB Relationship is an ideal way to get the business off the ground.

Gaining access to a time-crafted list of potential clients in your target market is an impressive benefit. Getting an established business to communicate your offer on your behalf is an almost guaranteed way to establish your own credibility.

However, start-ups often have the least to offer a 'host' company in exchange for being the 'beneficiary'. Trading client lists is not an option in this case. So what's in it for the 'host'?

The host is seen in the eyes of his customers as providing a reward or an exclusive offer for their continued support and loyalty. The host business earns goodwill and has an excuse to contact his database for the cost of a simple mailing.

**2. Entering a New Market**

An established business venturing into new territory is in a prime position to benefit from a HB Relationship. Whether the business is known or unknown in the community, tapping into a refined target list will ensure that the right people are communicated the benefits of the new business' offering.

In exchange, the host business may benefit from either the beneficiary's client lists in other marketplaces, or the prestige of offering clients an exclusive offer for a new business in town.

Again, this works best when the target market is highly segmented; otherwise, an advertisement would be a faster and more cost effective strategy.

**3. A New Product / Service**

As with new marketplaces, launching a new product or service may require tapping into a new or more segmented audience to deliver your message. A HB Relationship with the right partner will help to correctly position your offering, and deliver it to an exact audience.

The host business benefits by offering loyal clients the first opportunity to purchase or use the beneficiary business' product or service.

## Defining Your Target Market

This is crucial in establishing a HB Relationship – just like it is crucial in every other aspect of your marketing plan. Not knowing and understanding your target market will put you on the fast track to business hardship, and waste time and money in the process.

You can determine your target market – or target market segment – based on the purpose or intention for seeking a HB Relationship. Are you reaching out to a new segment of your market? Are you offering a new product or service that may appeal to a specific segment of your market? Are you moving to a new market area and looking to establish yourself amongst your broader target?

Determine your audience and write your target market here:

______________________________________________________________

______________________________________________________________

______________________________________________________________

**Selecting a Host Business**

Once you have an idea of who your target market is, you can begin to create a list of target host businesses to approach.

Not every business is going to be interested or willing to engage in this marketing strategy – so doing a little bit of research and positioning your offer is well worth your while. To begin, you will want to draft a long list of all potential host businesses.

Do this by considering all business types that would be complementary to – but not competing with – your fitness business.

Those businesses that offer a service or product that is connected in some way to your own. For example, if you operate a hair salon, some potential HB partners would include esthetics salons, clothing stores, drug stores, and perhaps some specialty goods stores.

Or, if you operate a retail tire store, you might consider a list that includes hardware stores, automotive part shops, car washes, auto body shops, or specialty auto part distributors.

Pick up the yellow pages, or conduct a Google search for all businesses in your market area that fall under the categories you identified. You may also consider asking your colleagues and associates for ideas and recommendations.

When creating this list, make sure each business falls under these criteria:

**Non-competitive.** Their offer should be complementary to, but not compete with, your product or service. Make sure you consider this carefully – seemingly non-competitive offers may actually cannibalize your business.

Remember that your customers have a limited amount of money to spend, and if they begin spending money at your host's business, they might stop spending money at your business.

**Same target market.** If you and your host business are not talking to the same customer base, then you're wasting your words on customers who are not likely to buy your service or product. If your host business has no idea who their target market is, you may also want to consider looking at other host options.

Start with your customers – your target market or segment of. What services do they use? What products are they interested in? Thinking about their needs will help lead you to the most effective host business.

**A killer customer contact list.** Without this, they aren't worth approaching – but how do you know they have or maintain a customer database? There are a couple of ways. Pay attention to the type of marketing your potential host conducts. Do they often send letters to their target market? Direct-mail flyers and other promotional materials? Or do they rely on advertising? Do they send a regular newsletter? They also may hold their customer contact information in their point of sale system – if it is technologically advanced enough to do so.

**Positive reputation.** As the beneficiary, you need to ensure that the host who is referring your business to their customers enjoys a good reputation in the community and with its clientele. Otherwise, you are being endorsed by a business that no one respects, which can be damaging for your reputation.

## Host Business Ideas List

Keep track of all potential host businesses using this chart.

| Business Name | Contact | Business Type |
|---|---|---|
| | Name:<br>Phone: | |
| | Name:<br>Phone: | |
| | Name:<br>Phone: | |
| | Name:<br>Phone: | |
| | Name:<br>Phone: | |
| | Name:<br>Phone: | |

| | | |
|---|---|---|
| | Name:<br>Phone: | |
| | Name:<br>Phone: | |

## Approaching the Host Business

Once you have created a list of target businesses, it is time to plan your approach. There is some strategy involved in this; you need to convince the host businesses to lend their endorsement and customer contact list to you in exchange for something that will benefit them.

**Introduce your product or service**. Present your offering to the host business as though you were presenting to your potential customers: heavy on benefits, and light on features. Assume that the host business has placed themselves in the shoes of their customers, and is evaluating whether your product or service is worthwhile for them.

Provide marketing materials and other supporting information like testimonials and market research to establish your credibility, and your understanding of the people you are trying to reach.

**Inform and excite**. Provide as much information about how the HB Relationship will work, and be sincere in your efforts. Leave room for their thoughts and contributions to ensure that they buy into the process.

Get them excited about the opportunity you've placed in front of them. Use bright examples, and tell a hypothetical story about one of their customers benefiting from your service. Then, bring it back to the benefits that the relationship or partnership will deliver to their business.

**Include an incentive**. Be clear about the benefits the host can expect to receive. While you will not always be able to offer something tangible, do your best to offer some incentive to the prospective host business.

If you are an established business, offer them reverse access to your customer database after the initial mailing. Or, if you have room in your margin, offer them a piece of the profits you receive from their customers. Whatever it is, make sure you articulate how this particular partnership is worth their while.

**Communicate your rationale**. Tell the host why you chose to approach them in particular. Do they enjoy a great reputation in the community? Are they a well-known business with a great sense of camaraderie? Compliment them on their business skills and the great relationships they have built with their customers and in the community.

Then, explain how your business can add value to theirs, and allow them to build on the existing relationships with their clients by offering your services.

**Reassure**. Communicate the benefits of the HB Relationship to the host, and reassure them that there is no risk involved for them. You are not out to take their profits, or place burden on their resources.

Remind them that you are seeking a complementary business relationship, one that benefits both parties.

## Craft Your Message

Once you have secured your host partner, put the plan into action as quickly as possible. Offering to write the letter to their customers will not only give you control over the messaging of the offer, but also reduce the time investment required by the host. The process is simplified for them, and happens sooner for you.

- Just like sales letters and other marketing collateral, your HB offer letter should engage the reader and make them feel as though their needs and interests are cared for.
- The letter should position the host as a thoughtful service provider who sought out an offer specifically for the target audience.
- Your offer should be strong and slightly outrageous. Give deep discounts, or free services, exclusively to this target audience.
- Remember to acknowledge the needs and troubles of your reader, and position your product or service as the answer or solution.
- Include an incentive to act quickly. Ensure your offer is time-sensitive or of limited quantity.

## Five Simple Steps to Creating an HB Relationship

In summary, here are is a five-step roadmap to creating a positive, profit-filled, HB Relationship:

- Identify your target market.
- Identify target host businesses.
- Create a unique offer for each host business.
- Approach the host business.

## Draft your letter.

## Points to Remember

- **Make mistakes in small batches.** If you are unsure about the accuracy of your target market – do a test run. Send a small batch of 50-100 letters to a small group of people, and measure the response.
  - Alternately, you can send three different letters to each third of your target market, and evaluate which offer is acted on the most. This is of benefit for both the host and the beneficiary business because the response rate of the target market is tested, as are their purchase motivations.
- **Create benefit for the host business.** Remember that there must be an incentive for the host business, or the partnership is not worth the time investment. It is important to consider this, and plan ahead before you approach the host business. Create a number of options for the host to choose from, whether it is using your database after the initial mailing, or sharing a piece of the profits.
- **Be honest.** If you are working with several businesses in your area on different offers, make sure each business knows and is comfortable with the arrangement. Ensure that each offer is distinctive and each host is benefiting from the arrangement without competing with other host businesses. This is just good business form.
- **Rest on the strength of your offer.** With a strong offer, your HB campaign will be on the path to success. Make it something your audience can't refuse. Your offer should not only be enticing and engaging for your audience, but should also benefit the host in reputation. Their customers should feel valued and appreciative toward the host for bringing your offer forward.

- **Repeat.** Once you've stablished one successful HB partnership, keep going! This technique is a valuable way to promote your business and your unique products and services, and can be repeated several times each year with several different host businesses.

## Host Beneficiary Letter Template

***[Headline in bold at the top of the page – strong statement or question]***

*[Optional sub headline to explain or answer the question/statement]*

*Dear [name],*

*I hope this letter finds you well and enjoying [insert name or description of product or service previously purchased]. Remember, your continued satisfaction with our [product or service] is guaranteed.*

*I am writing because I have stumbled upon an exclusive new [product or service] that will [describe how the product or service will meet a need or solve a problem].*

*[Beneficiary business name] is a [describe business type] that [describe business function]. I recently met with the owner, and was able to secure an unbelievable rate for my existing clients. The [product or service] is [describe product or service briefly]. Customers who have already purchased have said:*

*[list testimonials in bullet form]*

*[describe limited time or quantity], we are pleased to offer you [describe unique offer here]. This is an opportunity you will not find anywhere else, and an offer that will not be available in stores.*

*I hope you will be able to take advantage of this amazing [product or service].*

*Sincerely,*

*[your name]*

*[company name]*

*[phone number]*

## HB Relationship Worksheet

| | | |
|---|---|---|
| **Target Market:** | | |
| **Potential Host 1:**<br>Name:<br>Business Type: | **Unique Offer:** | |
| **Host Benefits:** | **Date Contacted:** | |
| | ☐ Accepted | ☐ Follow-up |
| **Notes:** | | |
| **Target Market:** | | |
| **Potential Host 2:**<br>Name:<br>Business Type: | **Unique Offer:** | |
| **Host Benefits:** | **Date Contacted:** | |
| | ☐ Accepted | ☐ Follow-up |
| **Notes:** | | |

# So What Do You Do From Here?

Take Action! If you're already an accomplished fitness business owner and earning in excess of $250,000.00 per year (rich according to the Federal Government), use this book as direction to enhance the speed of your business success. If you are not as accomplished as you would like to be then the smartest thing to do is…

A) Concentrate on strategies to LEARN and the EARN will follow! If you are serious about taking the next step then go to work on yourself, study other fitness business successes, understand marketing strategies and become a sponge for new (proven) material. The amazing thing about the game of business is that when you put proven processes to work and continue to follow them, an abundance of success will follow. The biggest mistake is to start a process and then fallback into your old habits after a short time.

B) Above all, get the knowledge you need before you step onto the field. Think about it… if you were going to challenge Garry Kasparov to a game of Chess for money, wouldn't it make sense to learn the game and the strategies and practice before you sat down to play him? It is amazing to me how many fitness business owners start the game of business against seasoned professionals (the competition), without first developing the necessary knowledge to be successful. Then they fail and blame the market, the economy, their location, etc.

C) If you have a fitness business and have not yet managed to start to create wealth and systems that allow you to take time off, build retirement accounts or pay for your children's college, then learn and master the steps outlined in my book. I am a huge advocate of education and mentorships. Get the right information, find someone that knows how to walk you through them and watch your quality of life take new shape.

For a Free Test Drive of all my best tips, tricks and marketing resources, visit www.shockexpert.com and/or www.ficonsult.net

www.ingramcontent.com/pod-product-compliance
Lightning Source LLC
Chambersburg PA
CBHW070046210526
45170CB00012B/599
*9781545167724*